LIVING FAITH

TONY CASTLE

Living Faith

An Introduction to Catholic Spirituality

ST PAULS

ST PAULS Publishing
187 Battersea Bridge Road, London SW11 3AS, UK
www.stpaulspublishing.com

Copyright © ST PAULS, 2009

ISBN 978-0-85439-747-1

Set by Tukan DTP, Stubbington, Fareham, UK
Printed and bound in Great Britain by Athenaeum Press Ltd,
Gateshead, Tyne & Wear

ST PAULS is an activity of the priests and brothers
of the Society of St Paul who proclaim the Gospel
through the media of social communication

*Dedicated to
The Rt. Rev. Thomas McMahon,
Bishop of Brentwood,
in gratitude
for thirty years of kindness and support.*

'In life's various styles, ways and duties, one and the same holiness is cultivated by all who are moved by the Spirit of God, and who obey the voice of the Father, worshipping God the Father in spirit and in truth. These people follow the poor Christ, the humble and cross-bearing Christ, in order to be made worthy of being partakers in His glory. Every person should walk unhesitatingly according to his own personal gifts and duties in the path of a living faith which arouses hopes and works through charity.'

Para 39, Chapter 5, *The Call to Holiness*,
Constitution, The Church: The Second Vatican Council.

CONTENTS

Introduction		9
Chapter 1	The Time Capsule	15
Chapter 2	What is Spirituality?	24
	St Thérèse of Lisieux	32
Chapter 3	The Eucharistic Centre	35
	St Margaret Clitherow	40
Chapter 4	The Word of God	44
	St Augustine of Hippo	52
Chapter 5	The Witness of Scripture	56
	St Jerome	63
Chapter 6	Authority and Guidance	65
	St Francis de Sales	71
Chapter 7	Repentance and Baptism	73
	St John Vianney	81
Chapter 8	The Hidden Presence	85
	St Benedict Labre	92
Chapter 9	Cross or Crucifix?	94
	Blessed Dominic Barberi	99
Chapter 10	Mary, the Mother of God	103
	St Bernadette	112
Chapter 11	The Saints	115
	Pope John Paul II	122
Chapter 12	Heart of Love	126
	St John Eudes	132
Chapter 13	The Liturgical Year	134
	St Nicholas	142
Chapter 14	Developments in Catholic Spirituality	145
	St Maria Faustina	151
Chapter 15	Out into the World	155
	Blessed Frederic Ozanam	162
Glossary		165

Appendix One: The Great Spiritual Guides and Writers	191
Appendix Two: Some False Spiritual Paths	202
Appendix Three: Apparitions of the Blessed Virgin Mary	205
Appendix Four: Catholic Spirituality: The Impact of the Second Vatican Council	215
Appendix Five: Recusant Teaching Songs	218
Appendix Six: Patron Saints	222
Bibliography	228
Index	231

INTRODUCTION

Life's spiritual dimension

Golden autumn leaves, spectacular blood-red sunsets, breathtaking snow-capped mountain scenery; who can fail to appreciate and be stirred by the beauty found in Nature? Appreciating Nature's beauties, and valuing beauty itself, and other values like truth, integrity, humility and unselfish love, lead us unerringly to the life of the Spirit, whether we are 'religious' or not. There is a spiritual dimension to life and every individual's life; this is acknowledged by atheists and agnostics. In his *In God We Doubt*,[1] John Humphrys, of BBC Radio 4 fame, writes, 'there remains what the atheist philosopher, A.C. Grayling calls, "the lingering splinter in the mind... a sense of yearning for the absolute." There is a profound longing for something that will stimulate and satisfy emotionally and spiritually. Grayling, and other atheists, understand that longing perfectly well, but what puzzles them is why it cannot be satisfied by pottering about in the garden, a walk in the hills, watching a sunset.' For Christians 'that longing' finds satisfaction in a faith-filled life, and it always remains as a prompt or goad to seek ever deeper and closer union with God.

Spirituality Matters

There can be no Christian spirituality without a living faith, some appreciation of the love of God and a full acceptance of God's revelation in and through Jesus Christ. This realisation was driven home to me when, visiting relatives in Suffolk I picked up a free magazine, which caught my eye, in the local store, called *Spirituality Matters*. After browsing through it, I had to acknowledge that the only agreement I would be able to reach with the editor and sole contributor, would be in the two-word title. Spirituality does matter; but the critical question is, what do you understand by 'spirituality'? This question we explore, in some depth, in chapter two, because the word 'spirituality' carries different meanings for different people. The promotional material, for the magazine that I picked up, excitedly reported that their new astrologer was also a Reiki Master, a Seicham Master, a Clairvoyant, a Clairaudient and Medium! The latest issue, the banner heading proclaimed, would also include articles by a woman who is a Wican Priestess and Elder of the Guardnarian Tradition! (One could be forgiven for imagining that readers were to be led through the fantasy world of the *Lord of the Rings*.) 'Spirituality', the editor authoritatively informs us in the editorial column, is 'all about love and compassion and doing things you know in your heart to be right because you want to do them'.

Christian Spirituality

The words 'love' and 'compassion' mean much to all Christians but, from the Christian position, there are serious problems about any 'spirituality' that is, first of all, not based upon a living faith; which includes no mention of God's immeasurable love for us and our poor efforts, with His aid, to respond to that love, and a compassion, and a moral conduct, that springs from this and God's revelation in Christ. The editorial column of *Spirituality Matters*, written under the banner heading 'Religion: Part of the Problem not the Solution', revealed that the 'spirituality' promoted by this magazine is violently opposed to all forms of organised religion and appears to accept the reality of 'spirits and angels,' but no personal God!

Approaches to the Christian traditions

There are various possible ways of introducing interested readers to Christian Spirituality; one could be historical, like Simon Tugwell's *Ways of Imperfection* (1984) tracing the development of spirituality since the time of the Apostles. Another could be thematical, as in Alister E. McGrath's *Christian Spirituality* (1999), exploring types, theology and themes. However, the subject, covering 2,000 years and the three different traditions, of Catholic, Protestant and Orthodox, is so vast that a simple introduction would either be too shallow or too complex and therefore of no real value to the enquiring reader. One popular thought provoking attempt by Richard Foster in his *Streams of Living Water* (1999) identifies seven streams, or spiritual traditions in Christianity, and traces and explores them. However the book does not include the Orthodox tradition and, from the Catholic perspective, there appears to be a lack of balance in the presentation of the seven streams.

Spirituality for all

Traditionally the average Catholic has regarded 'the spiritual life' and 'spirituality' as the province and sole concern of priests, nuns and monks. This misconception was tackled by the Second Vatican Council (whose authoritative documents will be constantly referred to in this book). The central and most important document of the Council was the Constitution on the Church; the centre of the document is chapter 5 entitled 'The Call of the Whole Church to Holiness'. Here are a few relevant sentences from that important chapter:

> 'The Lord Jesus, the Divine Teacher and Model of all perfection, preached holiness of life to each and every one of His disciples, regardless of their situation.'

'It is evident to everyone that all the faithful of Christ, of whatever rank or status are called to the fullness of the Christian life and to the perfection of charity. By this holiness a more human way of life is promoted even in this earthly society' (para 40).

'All of Christ's followers, therefore, are invited and bound to pursue holiness and the perfect fulfilment of their proper state in life' (para 42).[2]

So 'the spiritual life' and 'spirituality' are not optional extras for Catholics.

Presenting Catholic Spirituality

Catholic Spirituality, in itself, is a huge subject and it too can be approached historically or thematically, but I believe that a much more interesting and 'hands-on' approach is to introduce interested readers to the spiritual life of the Catholic Church by way of what can actually be seen, touched and experienced in the average parish church. Just by entering a Catholic church, one is entering into a kind of 'time-capsule,' which, when examined, reveals the centrality of the liturgy on the one hand and the devotional life of the people on the other. Apart from chapter two, which explores 'What is Spirituality?' each chapter has a 'focus point', which is a feature or artefact to be found in the church building. This could be the altar, a statue or the church notice board; each has much to teach us about the spiritual life of the community that gathers for worship in that parish church.

Fourteen Saints

The spirituality we are exploring, in this simple introduction to a vast topic, is primarily about 'persons', not feelings or fantasies. From the love life of the three persons of the Blessed Trinity, to the forgiving of others and loving our neighbour, it is all relational. Church ritual, penitential practices and devotional services are only of value in the context of the love of God, neighbour and oneself. ('You must love the Lord your God with all your heart, with all your soul, with all your strength, and with all your mind, and your neighbour as yourself' [Lk 10:27].) The saints are those who have been acknowledged by the Church to be heroic models of this demanding Christian way of life. For this reason each chapter (apart from the first) is 'fleshed out' with a short life of a saint, who relates particularly to the content of that chapter.

Using this book

The content of each chapter is centred around something that can be seen in a Catholic church, for example, the focus for chapter 4 is the Ambo. This focus is clearly identified at the start of each chapter. From the opening pages, when it is first used, any word or term, particular to Catholic life and practice, that may not be familiar to the general reader, is highlighted in **bold**. It is explained in full in the Glossary.

This book claims to be nothing more than the subtitle suggests, a simple introduction to Catholic Spirituality. While the writer has had the 'visitor' to the Spiritual life in mind, it is hoped that many, who are already familiar with much of the content, will find something that will nourish their living faith.

NOTES: INTRODUCTION

1. *In God We Doubt,* by John Humphreys, p.76.
2. The Second Vatican Council's Constitution on the Church, pp.67 and 72.

CHAPTER 1   *Focus:* THE CHURCH

THE TIME CAPSULE

Inside a Catholic church

To step into a Catholic **church** is to step into **Catholic Spirituality**. The regular churchgoer does not advert to it, but for the curious, first time visitor, the spiritual life of the community that worships there, is all around. Producers of films and television entertainment attempt to capture the spiritual atmosphere and ethos of Catholic churches by the use of subdued lighting and banks of burning candles. This attempt at authenticity can cause hilarity for thinking Catholics, who wonder how, in an empty church, so many candles can be so obviously freshly lit! But the very attempt reveals an awareness that there is something particularly different and special about this place of worship.

Church building – at a cost

The architecture and design of Catholic parish churches differ enormously, given that there were none in Britain before the middle of the nineteenth century. While a number of churches were built before the re-establishment of the Hierarchy for England and Wales in 1850, it was only when there were Bishops once again, did church-building really get under-way. There was the occasional rich benefactor, who could fund a Gothic church designed by Pugin (see below) or finance a number of basic church buildings. An example of the latter was the Ellis family, who purchased cheap land, alongside railway lines, in South-East London, at, for example, Nunhead, Peckham and Abbey Wood, and paid for the construction of simple, plain churches. However, most communities set about raising the money themselves, often building the parish school before the parish church. Since the great majority of Catholics, at that time, were to be found among the labouring classes, such an enterprise entailed considerable sacrifice, dedication and determination. The 'spirit' behind such a countrywide drive – now largely forgotten – by the fledgling English and Welsh Catholic Church was a powerful witness to the Spirituality, which informed it. Every one of those nineteenth- and early-twentieth-century churches, purchased at great personal sacrifice and cost by innumerable devout parishioners, stands witness to their love of God and their Church.

Gothic Revival

In the 1840s the convert to Catholicism, Augustus Pugin (1812-1852), was at the height of his fame, as a much sought-after architect and leader of the style of architecture called 'the Gothic Revival'. Among Pugin's works are St Chad's Cathedral, Birmingham, (completed in 1841); St Giles, Cheadle, (completed in 1846); St Augustine's Abbey, Ramsgate, (completed in 1851). Some Catholic communities positively rejected Pugin's identification of Gothic, as the purest form of Christian architecture, preferring instead Italian designs and styles. In reality, most ordinary Catholic parishes could not rise to an expensive church in the Gothic Revival style and settled for the best they could afford.

One representative lay example

Listed in Appendix One are the names of some of the significant spiritual writers, directors and guides of the last two thousand years, but it is the devotional life of the ordinary Christian that has ultimately borne witness to the spiritual life of the Catholic Church. People like Catherine Collins, of Great Wakering, in Essex, born in 1907, who, as a centenarian, was still bearing public witness by her cheerful faith-filled life in a Care home. When her two sons were small she would put them in a pushchair and walk the six miles to Sunday morning **Mass** at Shoeburyness, and back; then in the late afternoon, take the boys back to evening Rosary, Sermon and Benediction. When the bishop visited the parish she asked him for a church in the village of Great Wakering; he told her that he would approve one, if she could find the land and show that there were thirty-five families in the area, who would use the church. She approached a local farmer and pleaded her cause; he gave her the land, on condition that it was only ever used for a church. Mrs Collins then went from door to door of the large village, enquiring after the religious adherence of each family. She found over thirty-five Catholic (some only nominal) families and listed them. The bishop was full of admiration for her initiative, but asked how it was going to be funded. Cathy Collins had thought about that and told him that she was going to call weekly on each Catholic family and collect a donation. So impressed were the families that none failed to support her. The church was blessed and opened by the bishop in June 1963. (Although over fifty people were regularly attending Mass each weekend at St Edmund's, Mrs Collins was devastated when the shortage of priests caused it to be closed in September 1995.)

A representative clerical example

What happened in south-east Essex, in the Southend-on-Sea area, is a good illustration of how the Catholic Church in England and Wales grew swiftly from very poor beginnings. The following is by Alfred P. Goodale writing in the *Essex Countryside*, April 1976.

Southend's first resident Roman Catholic priest, Fr John Moore, watched a revolutionary mob erect a temporary scaffold outside the **Seminary** of St Sulpice in Paris, during the revolutionary uprising of 1829. John Moore was one of 200 students for the Priesthood at the seminary and the power-drunk revolutionaries made it quite clear that the first victims on their scaffold would be the students and their priests. When the mob stormed the building and paraded the students in front of the scaffold they undoubtedly thought their end had come. But young John Moore was a powerfully-built Irishman and he pushed his way to the leader of the mob and exclaimed: "It was the Irish who won the battle of Fontenoy for you and I am an Irishman."

"That's true", replied the leader. "What is it you want?" Moore replied, "I want the lives of my fellow students and those who teach us." After consulting the other revolutionary leaders, many of whom wanted to kill the young Catholics, it was eventually decided that if Moore, with the other students, would march through the streets of Parish carrying the red flag and singing the Marseillaise, they would escape death.

Moore spoke to the students who agreed to the terms of their release. They fulfilled their side of the bargain by parading through the streets, singing the Marseillaise, led by Moore who carried a red flag. While they were doing that the scaffold was dismantled. The students dispersed and after their training many of them served on 'the English Mission'.

John Moore was ordained priest and came to England. He built the mission church of St Mary and St Michael, in Commercial Road in the East End of London; then his bishop moved him to Wapping where he oversaw the building of a church and school. In April 1862 he arrived in Southend-on-Sea, which was rapidly developing, from a fishing village into a health resort. There was no Catholic church in the whole area so Fr Moore took a house in Capel Terrace, which was one of the newer thoroughfares in the area. He decided to start a Catholic mission in his home and he celebrated his first Mass in Southend in an upstairs room on 1 May 1862. He later recalled that his first congregation in Southend consisted of an old and faithful servant, a small boy and a relative!

There was little money to promote his mission and Fr Moore's poverty was aggravated by his charity. In 1864 he was forced to write to his bishop asking for help to pay the rent. It was his quiet but energetic ministry that attracted the attention of the Countess Tasker, while on holiday in Southend. She was so impressed that she told Fr Moore she would pay for the site of a church, school and presbytery. Land was found in Milton Road, Westcliff-on-Sea, (close to Southend) and it was a great day when the Countess, on 8 October 1868, laid the foundation stone of the Church of Our Lady and St Helen. Unfortunately Lady Tasker died before the completion of the church, school and presbytery. Today three Catholic parishes, with their churches (average Mass attendance at each is 550 people) and schools, serve the same area of Fr Moore's mission in the mid-nineteenth century'.

Pre- and Post-Vatican Council II

Surveying the Catholic churches built in England and Wales in the last two centuries there is a general divide between churches built before the Second Vatican Council (1962-1965) and those that were constructed with the liturgical principles of that Council in mind. The former, built in the traditional style, with long, narrow naves, have been re-ordered to accommodate, as well as possible, the liturgical reforms promoted by the Council. However, whether old or new, all Catholic churches have many common features. In fact, each church is like a time capsule of Church History. There are foundational links with the Early Church of the first centuries of Christianity, devotional aids from the Middle Ages and more recent devotions, like statues of the Sacred Heart of Jesus and Our Lady of Lourdes or of Fatima. The universal Church does not, and has never, lived in a sacred vacuum divorced from the styles and fashions of, what is for every generation, 'modern' living. This is equally true of the Catholic spirituality of the past. In every church, even recently constructed ones, there are historical links with the Catholics of the past and their cherished spirituality.

Evolving Spirituality

Cardinal John Henry Newman, (1801-1890) a convert from Anglicanism and a contemporary of Charles Darwin, wrote his famous *The Development of Christian Doctrine*, almost immediately after his reception into the Catholic Church in 1845. In it he applied the principles of evolution (although Darwin had not published his evidence yet, evolution was already widely discussed) to how Christian doctrine had, under the direction and guidance of the Holy Spirit, evolved and developed from Apostolic times. The same is true of Spirituality; it has developed and evolved over many centuries. Thanks to the constant presence and working of the Holy Spirit, we are richer now in the knowledge, understanding and appreciation of the Spiritual Life than were our predecessors in the Faith. Just as scientists working today on, for example, stem cell research, are totally dependent upon the years and years of patient and dedicated research of earlier scientists, so too our modern spiritual guides, writers, confessors and directors draw upon the wisdom of the spiritual writers and guides of the past (see Appendix Two).

Altar – the focal point

The focal point of every Catholic church is the **altar**. In theory the building could be emptied of everything else: the **font**, the **stations of the cross**, the **tabernacle** etc. Nothing (apart from the ambo) compares to the altar in importance; its presence makes it an authentic Catholic place of worship. The building would not be a 'church' if the local Catholic community could not celebrate there the Mass. As will be clear from the notes in the Glossary, in a nutshell, the place where Catholics meet to celebrate the Eucharist is called '*a* church', because '*the* Church' meet there. So, if the community were meeting each week in a large room for Mass above a supermarket (as they did for some years in Tunbridge Wells, in Kent) that is their 'church'.

Ambo, of equal importance

Standing alongside, quite close to the altar, is the next most important feature, the **ambo**, or **lectern**. The activity that takes place here – the reading and proclamation of Sacred Scripture – is of parallel importance to what takes place on the altar. That is because the Mass consists of the two parts, the liturgy of the Eucharist, preceded by the liturgy of the Word of God.

Sedilia, presider's chair

After these two, the next feature of the church building of importance is the celebrant's chair; in medieval times identified with the **sedilia**. This seat is reserved for the presiding priest, who is appointed by the local bishop and officiates in his name; however in the actual celebration of the community, he represents Christ. These three features, the altar, the ambo and the celebrant's chair, originate from the earliest days of the Church. The other features, like the font and the tabernacle, are of later development. In the following chapters we will explore how they not only reveal the various stages of Church history, but also the development of Catholic spirituality over the centuries.

Down-to-earth Spirituality

The spirituality that we are considering in this book is not theoretical and ethereal, it is real and down-to-earth; it is person-centred. In this first chapter we have 'met' Mrs Cathy Collins, Fr John Moore and Cardinal John Henry Newman; an ordinary housewife, a busy parish priest and an academic, who, in the last few years of his life was elevated to the highest ranks of the Roman Catholic Church. Each was inspired and 'driven' by their faith; each was a deeply spiritual person. It is in the lives of faith-filled people that we can witness what authentic Catholic spirituality is. Each of the following chapters will close with a short life, relevant to that chapter, of one of the spiritual heroes of the past; one of the saints.

SUMMARY

The parish church is the spiritual home of the local Catholic community. In the late nineteenth and early-twentieth centuries, after 300 years of persecution, when English legislation permitted, many sacrifices were made to provide churches for the communities of England and Wales. Churches built before 1965 are traditional in design, after that date the reforming decrees of the Second Vatican Council (1962-1965) occasioned a change in building design to make the liturgy more accessible to lay people. However, all Catholic churches have basically the same features; these we explore in the coming pages.

CHAPTER 2

WHAT IS SPIRITUALITY?

The Spiritual Dimension

Aggressive atheism is in vogue. Books by eminent atheists top the book charts while sincere doubters, like the renowned broadcaster, John Humphrys, (of BBC's Radio 4) disturb believers and non-believers alike. However in his best-seller, *In God We Doubt,* Humphrys admits that 'there is what the atheist, A.C. Grayling calls 'the lingering splinter in the mind ... a profound longing for something that will stimulate and satisfy emotionally and spiritually'. Later he writes, 'Jean-Paul Sartre's conclusion, in *The Age of Reason* that "there is no purpose to existence, only nothingness" is a perfectly rational conclusion if you cannot accept that we exist in order to worship God. But, however much he may appeal to our reason, Sartre's conclusion is too bleak for me. Trite it may be, but most of us can see the beauty as well as the horrors of the world and, sometimes, humanity at its most noble. We sense a spiritual element in that nobility and, in the miracle of unselfish love and sacrifice, something beyond our conscious understanding. You don't need to be an eastern mystic or a devout religious believer to feel that.'[1]

Fashionable Spirituality

Was it the visit of the Beatles to the Maharishi, in Rishikesh, India, in 1968 that launched the modern interest in 'spirituality'? Certainly, despite and in the face of a tide of aggressive atheism, there has been a remarkable growth in interest in the whole area of spirituality in recent years. In many quarters there is a frustrated cynicism with the failure of money and the accumulation of possessions to provide lasting satisfaction, fulfilment and peace, which has led to a much greater attention being paid to the spiritual dimensions of life. Spirituality is in fashion. Side by side with a gradual decline in church attendance and the appeal of any form of institutionalised religion, there has been a discernible rise in popular interest in spirituality. Christian leaders and teachers have, too often, felt that people, searching for spiritual values and answers to life's deep questions, have looked to the East, the New Age Movement and to more esoteric forms, rather than explore and appreciate that Christianity, and particularly Catholicism, has a deep, rich and mature spirituality, shaped over 2,000 years.

A Faith-filled life

But what is 'spirituality'? In general – before we look at 'Catholic' spirituality – it carries a wide and often ill defined meaning. It is used to refer to people's subjective practice and experience of their religion, or to the spiritual exercises and beliefs which individuals or groups have with regard to their personal relationship with God.

The word 'spiritualitas' first appears in the fifth century, but it draws on the Hebrew word *ruach,* usually translated as 'spirit'. 'To talk about "the spirit" is to discuss what gives life and animation to someone, 'Spirituality' is thus about the life of faith – what drives and motivates it, and what people find helpful in sustaining and developing it.'[2] So a basic definition of 'Spirituality' might be:

> Spirituality concerns the quest for a fulfilled and authentic religious life, involving the bringing together of the ideas distinctive of that religion and the whole experience of living on the basis of and within the scope of that religion.

Richard O'Brien, in *Catholicism,* says that 'Spirituality has to do with our experiencing God and with the transformation of our consciousness and our lives as outcomes of that experience.'[3]

Inclusive of Christ

For the Christian, 'experiencing God' means encountering and responding to Jesus the Christ. So Christian spirituality concerns the living out of the encounter with Jesus; of living the call to discipleship to the full. Two modern writers can help us to a fuller appreciation of what we mean by 'Christian spirituality' or 'the spiritual life'. First, Evelyn Underhill, the Anglican Spiritual writer, revered as a saint by the Episcopal Church of USA, whose BBC broadcasts were extremely popular in the 1930s.

> 'The 'spiritual life' is a dangerously ambiguous term; indeed it would be interesting to know what meaning any one reader, at the present moment, is giving to these three words. Many, I am afraid, would really be found to mean 'the life of my own inside'; and a further section, to mean something very holy, difficult and peculiar – a sort of honours degree course in personal religion – to which they did not intend to aspire.
>
> Both these kinds of individualist – the people who think of the spiritual life as something which is for themselves and about themselves, and the people who regard it as something which is not for themselves – seem to need a larger horizon, within which these interesting personal facts can be placed; seen in rather truer proportion. Any spiritual view which focuses attention on ourselves, and puts the human creature with its small ideas and adventures in the centre foreground, is dangerous until we recognise its absurdity.'[4]

The second passage is from Amy Welborn, who is a popular modern spiritual writer from Indiana, USA.

> 'I'm starting to wonder about the air I breath. The spiritual air, that is, the air that's drifting around my culture's definition of what the spiritual life is all about. Because in that air there is an assumption that my spiritual life is essentially about me: about finding peace, a space where I feel accepted and comfortable. But when I actually go back to the sources – to, for example, Paul writing to the Christians of Corinth (2 Cor 8:9) 'Our Lord Jesus Christ became poor although he was rich, so that by his poverty you might become rich' – we find Paul encouraging the Corinthians to pour out more of themselves in love, because their redemption came as Christ poured himself out for them – I have to think again. It almost seems to be a different language sometimes. Joy and peace are the fruit of the journey, but the name of the journey might be something different from what some of us think. It might not be so much, 'The way to inner peace', but simply, 'Discipleship'.[5]

Catholic Spirituality

Catholic Spirituality is based firmly upon 'Discipleship'; the following of the Master, Jesus the Saviour. But what did Christ bring that was not there before? What does he bring us that is distinctive from the spirituality of other World Religions? Pope Benedict XVI in his *Jesus of Nazareth* provides the answer:

> 'He has not brought world peace, and he has not conquered the world's misery. So he can hardly be the true Messiah, who after all, is suppose to do just that. Yes, what has Jesus brought? He has brought

us God. He has brought the God of Israel to the nations, so that all the nations now pray to him and recognise Israel's Scriptures as his word, the word of the living God. He has brought the gift of universality, which was the one great definitive promise to Israel and the world. This universality, this faith in the one God of Abraham, Isaac and Jacob – extended now in Jesus' new family to all nations over and above the bonds of descent according to the flesh – is the fruit of Jesus' work.'[6]

Jesus' new family

Pope Benedict XVI, in simply referring to the Church as 'Jesus' new family', places the discipleship we have spoken of in the context of the community of the Baptised. Christians are not individuals seeking salvation on their own, first and foremost they are members of the Body of Christ (Col 1:24). The Christian's spiritual life – life in the Spirit – commences in the waters of Baptism:

> 'For we were all baptised by one Spirit into one body – whether Jews or Greeks, slave or free – and we were all given the one Spirit to drink' (1 Cor 12:13).

Catholic spirituality is, therefore, distinctly different from independently 'doing things you know in your heart to be right' (see the Introduction), for it is the search for union with God, in and through Christ Jesus, by the power and inspiration of the Holy Spirit, as experienced in and through the sacramental life of Jesus' new family, the Church.

Sacramental Church

Christian Churches are generally regarded as belonging to one of three different traditions; Catholic, Protestant or Orthodox. There is, perhaps, a clearer divide between Sacramental and Non-sacramental Churches; that is those who regard the **Sacraments** as essential to the Spiritual life – Catholic, Anglican (the Catholic wing of the Anglican Communion) and Orthodox – and those who do not; for example, the Baptists, Pentecostals and many other Christian groups, who would identify themselves as 'Bible Christians'. (We shall see how important the Scriptures are to Catholics in chapters 4 and 5.)

The Centrality of the Incarnation

It was, for the Apostles, the earth-shattering, humanly unbelievable, Resurrection of Christ from the tomb, that changed everything for them and revealed to them the divinity of Christ. It was the Resurrection event (hence, for Catholics, the centrality of Easter) that revealed that the Messiah was not just another great preacher and miracle-working prophet, but truly God himself among them. The Evangelist John was later to describe this in his famous words, 'The Word became flesh, he lived among us, and we saw his glory, the glory that he has from his Father as only Son of the Father' (Jn 1:14). The wondrous Christian belief – quite staggering if one stops to dwell on it – that the eternal, all mighty God should enter into, and become totally identified with his human creatures, living on a tiny planet, tucked away in a corner of the Milky Way Galaxy – just one of the millions of galaxies in his universe – is the foundation belief of Christianity. Called 'the Incarnation' (originating from the words, 'The Word became flesh'), this belief is central to an understanding of the Sacraments (see Glossary) and Catholic Spirituality.

The Indwelling of Christ

The Catholic's spiritual life, beginning with Baptism, can develop, with God's grace, from the external observances of regular church membership to a greater closeness to Christ. Regular reception of the Sacraments, an ordered prayer life and reading the Scriptures, can develop into an awareness of God's continual presence – what is called 'the practice of the Presence of God'. This can mature (with a dependence, all the while, on the active presence of the Holy Spirit) to an appreciation that the Risen Christ is not an external spiritual 'leader', but the lover who dwells within. (St Paul surely spoke of his own spiritual life when he wrote, 'it is no longer I, but Christ living in me... I am living in faith, faith in the Son of God who loved me and gave himself for me' [Gal 2:19].) And Paul prays for the Christians of Ephesus;

> 'In the abundance of his glory may he, through his Spirit, enable you to grow firm in power with regard to your inner self, so that Christ may live in your hearts through faith' (Eph 3:17).

Baptism, the starting point

Baptism, then, is the beginning of the spiritual journey for the Catholic; an illustration of this can be seen in the life of Pope John Paul II.

In the **presbytery**, across a narrow street from the parish church of Wadowice, Poland, in a simple visitors' room to the left of the front door, is a large safe. It contains the parish records and registers of the Baptisms, Marriages, etc of the local community. The register of baptisms, for the month of June, 1920, has an entry for the 20th, which is fuller than any other on that page or any other place in the register. Fortunately, or providentially, the entry is the last one on the right-hand page, which means that it was able to overflow into a spacious border. The entry records the baptism of one, Karol Joseph, son of Karol and Emilia Wojtyla, born on 18 May 1920. The original entry, like those above it, confidently occupies the centre of the allotted space. Where 'marriage' would normally be entered, there is 'priest' on 1.11.46. In smaller writing under that entry is 'Bishop' 28.9.58. Five years later, on 30th December, in even smaller writing is 'Archbishop of Cracow'. Then the margin has to be used for 'Cardinal' on 26.6.67. And finally in the last possible piece of margin is the entry, '16.10.78 in Summum Pontificem electus, Joannes Paulus II'.

The Spiritual life and journey of Pope John Paul II began on his baptismal day, 20 June 1920. Like very many others, baptised throughout Poland that day, he could have remained a nominal Catholic, with no desire to live the Baptismal promises made in his name by his godparents; or he could have rejected his Christian Faith completely. However, nurtured in a loving family that took the Catholic Faith seriously, although his mother died when he was six years old, Karol Wojtyla persevered and grew in faith and love of God. As a teenager he had to work as a slave, under the Nazi regime, in a stone quarry and a factory; but it was in that setting that his vocation to the priesthood was first experienced. He was not to know that it was God's plan that he should be bishop, then archbishop, cardinal and, finally, as Pope, one of the greatest spiritual leaders of the twentieth century. Now, in the early twenty-first century, his cause for sainthood has been put forward; but his spiritual journey began at the font of a parish church in a small market town in southern Poland.

The way to a deep spiritual life and great sanctity does not necessarily lie through exposure to the public eye, nor through difficult and complex methods. There is a very simple way, open to all, which was discovered and lived by a young French woman, St Thérèse of Lisieux, who lived her short life in almost total obscurity.

The Little Way to Sanctity
ST THÉRÈSE OF LISIEUX (1873-1897)

Thérèse, was the youngest of Louis and Zelie Martin's family of nine children, of whom only five survived childhood. Her father was a watchmaker and the family lived, quite comfortably, in Lisieux, Normandy, France. Her mother died of cancer when Thérèse was five and she was brought up by her older sisters. It was a very devout household, where prayer and the spiritual life were taken very seriously. (Louis Martin's cause for canonisation is going forward). Thérèse's four sisters left the family home, one by one, to become nuns; three of them joined the Carmelite convent in Lisieux. Thérèse, inspired by her sisters' example, was drawn towards the spiritual life from an early age. She began to agitate for her admission to the Carmelites at the age of 14 and, despite encountering much opposition, she persevered in pleading her vocation. Eventually she obtained permission to enter the convent at the age of 15. She was very happy in her religious life and took her final vows in 1890. She served the community as assistant novice-mistress and in 1896 she was bitterly disappointed when she was prevented from joining the Carmelites, in a missionary role, in China. She was prevented from going by the beginning of a series of haemorrhages, which was linked with tuberculosis.

As her illness painfully progressed the Mother Superior, Mother Agnes, (who was one of her sisters), instructed her to write her autobiography which she called, *L'Histoire d'une ame* (The Story of a Soul). In Thérèse's own mind the purpose of her story was to fulfil her mission in life. "My mission is to make God loved as I love Him, to teach souls my little way."[7] These words were written by Thérèse, when she was 24, just a few months before her death on 30 September 1897. When her sister, Mother Agnes of Jesus asked her, "And what is this little way you want to teach to souls?" Thérèse answered: "It is the way of spiritual childhood, the way of trust and absolute surrender." She had only ever had one desire, to be a saint, but, reading the lives of the great saints, Thérèse concluded that she could never be like them. It was not for her to achieve great works, convert thousands of non-believers and, perhaps, die a martyr's death. She said, "I can do one thing; I will be great in love"; and she was. Her 'Little Way', which anyone could imitate, was to love God and her neighbour with every tiny action of each day. Afflicted with tuberculosis Thérèse lived her spiritual life in continual severe pain; patiently and cheerfully she had a smile and a cheery word for everyone.

In her autobiography Thérèse often referred to herself as 'God's little flower' and this title, 'The Little Flower', became especially associated with her. Her book was a runaway international best-seller and thousands of pilgrims made the journey to Lisieux; and still do. Her popularity and appeal to the people of her time was largely due to her 'Little Way,' which revealed that the attainment of a full spiritual life, and even sanctity itself, was practicable through renunciation and loving in the small everyday matters and events of an ordinary life.

SUMMARY

The spiritual life of the Catholic is about living a life of faith, as a disciple of the Risen Christ, in his family, the Church. A faith-filled life is a Spirit-filled life. Spirituality, therefore, involves an openness to the work of the Holy Spirit, through the Word of God, prayer and meeting the Risen Christ, in and through the sacraments, starting with Baptism.

NOTES – CHAPTER 2

1. *In God We Doubt* by John Humphrys, quoted in the *Sunday Times*, 20 May 2007.
2. *Streams of Living Water* by Richard Foster, p.15.
3. *Christian Spirituality* by Alister E. McGrath, pp.2, 3.
4. *The Spiritual Life* by Evelyn Underhill, p.33.
5. *Living Faith,* Daily Devotions; an article by Amy Welborn, p.33.
6. *Jesus of Nazareth* by Pope Benedict XVI, p.116.
7. *Story of a Soul* by St Thérèse of Lisieux, p.XI.

CHAPTER 3   *Focus:* THE ALTAR

THE EUCHARISTIC CENTRE

Altar, focal point

It is obvious, on entering a Catholic church, that the altar is the focal point of the whole building. The Eucharist, that is conducted there, is the centre of the community's worship and prayer life. The Mass has, throughout history, evolved and developed, but, since the fourth century, the altar has been central in importance (although not always in position) and the community's symbol of unity. At the very beginning of the Church's existence, on the very day the Christian community came into being, 'the breaking of bread' (as the Eucharist was first called) is spoken of. Following Peter's speech, found in the Acts of the Apostles, we learn how, the converts 'devoted themselves to the apostles' teaching and to the fellowship, to the breaking of bread and to prayer (Acts 2:42).

And: 'Every day they continued to meet together in the temple courts. They broke bread in their homes and ate together with glad and sincere hearts' (Acts 2:46).

During the first century of the Christian era, 'the People of the Way', as Christians were first called (Acts 9:2, 16-18, 25-26), used one another's houses, or borrowed rooms as gathering places for the breaking of bread.

House churches

The ground floor plans of first century Roman villas, for example the Villa Anaploga in Corinth, or the house church excavated at Dura Europas, on the banks of the Euphrates, reveal dining rooms where Christians would gather for a communal meal. We learn from Paul's First Letter to the Christians of Corinth, chapter 11, that at the end of this meal, the Eucharist would be celebrated. There were no altars, only the triclinium – the three-sided arrangement for reclining on couches round a low wooden table. (We do not know for sure but it is likely that this was the arrangement at Christ's Last Supper with his friends.) We know, from St Paul's Letter to the Corinthians (11:17), that abuses had crept into these meals, which preceded the 'breaking of bread'. However the Eucharist was still faithfully celebrated.

Stone altars

When, and how, did stone altars replace wooden family tables? The answer is, as the result of the Roman persecutions. While the periods of persecution of the Christian Church were spasmodic and not continual, over a period of 250 years (64 to 313), they were a powerful influence in the shaping of the liturgy of the Christian community. Christians took refuge, from time to time, and conducted their worship in the 'catacombs'. These were a network of subterranean cemeteries that existed in many cities of the Empire. More than forty such cemeteries were dug outside the walls of Rome, as no burials were permitted in the city. Often consisting of three or four stories of underground passageways, the narrow corridors stretched for miles. Niches were cut from the floor to the ceiling to receive the bodies of the dead. Occasionally, these passages opened into small chapels, or burial chambers, for the more notable deceased person. It was in such a place that the body of a Christian hero, a martyr who had witnessed to the Faith, by undergoing vicious torture and brutal death, was laid to rest. Here, during times of persecution, the Christians would gather round the tomb, the top of which would be used as a table or altar. Naturally the tabletop would be stone and the length of a human body; because it was dark down there, a candle was placed at each end of the 'altar' top.

Relics under the altar

In 313 the Edict of Milan guaranteed religious freedom throughout the Empire and Constantine compensated the Christian community; partly with buildings that could be used as churches. The respect and honour given to the thousands of Christian heroes, who had died witnessing to their faith in Christ, had grown to such a degree that the bodies of the most popular of them were brought into the new churches and placed under the stone altar. As had been the custom in the catacombs, a candle was placed at each end of the tomb-length altar. Soon churches were being built all over Europe, and beyond, but there were not enough bodies of the most important of the martyrs to go round; so bones – **relics** – were made available. And still, today, 1,700 years later, altars in Catholic churches are of stone, the length of a human body and with relics of one of the early Christian martyrs sealed underneath. And the candles are still used!

Christ's words

From St Paul's words in his First Letter to the Corinthians, written some twenty-two years after Christ blessed and distributed, first the bread and then the wine, with the words, 'take and eat; this is my body' and 'this is my blood of the covenant' (Mt 26:26, 27), the Christian community's teaching on the Eucharist is clear:

> 'Anyone who eats the bread and drinks the cup of the Lord unworthily is answerable for the body and

blood of the Lord. Everyone is to examine himself and only then eat of the bread or drink from the cup; because a person who eats and drinks without recognising the body is eating and drinking his own condemnation' (1 Cor 11:28-29).

If this solemn warning is taken with the words of John, the Beloved Disciple, written about thirty-five years after St Paul's letter, the belief in the real presence of Christ in the Eucharist is evident.

'I am the living bread which has come down from heaven. Anyone who eats this bread will live for ever; and the bread that I shall give is my flesh, for the life of the world' (Ch 6:51).

'In all truth I tell you, if you do not eat the flesh of the Son of man and drink his blood, you have no life in you. Anyone who does eat my flesh and drink my blood has eternal life, and I shall raise that person up on the last day. For my flesh is real food and my blood is real drink. Whoever eats my flesh and drinks my blood lives in me and I live in that person' (Ch 6:53-56).

Such texts reveal why the Early Christians were prepared to risk their lives to hide in the catacombs to celebrate the Eucharist and why many Catholic heroes, through-out the centuries, have dedicated their lives to bringing the Mass to the people.

The real presence

The second passage from St John's Gospel uses the words 'life', 'live' or 'living' eight times. Christ is referring to the spiritual life, or the spirituality, of the believer. (Naturally the prerequisite for making sense of the above expression of Catholic belief is Faith). So it is not the observable, physical life of the believer that Jesus is making reference to, but the Christian's interior life of faith; his spiritual life.

In the second and third centuries of the Christian era, pagan Roman writers, encouraged by the Imperial authorities, mocked and derided the Christians for their 'cannibalism'; as they took literally the words of the New Testament. The populace expressed their incomprehension and rage with insulting graffiti on city walls. This is not surprising, because belief in the real, sacramental presence of Christ (not his physical bodily presence) in the Eucharist is dependent upon belief in the Resurrection. It is not the material, bodily presence of the first century man, who was carpenter, teacher, Messiah and Son of God, that is being referred to, but the mysterious, resurrected body of the glorified Christ. A presence that is real to his followers through the sacramental signs of the bread and wine in the Eucharist. This traditional teaching of the Catholic Church was clarified, by the Bishops of England and Wales, when they wrote in *One Bread, One Body*:

> 'Catholics believe that Christ in the Eucharist is "truly, really and substantially present". We can preserve intact our faith in this unique gift of Christ to his Church only by insisting on a change in the inner reality of the bread and the wine. Catholic teaching emphasises this conversion of the inner reality of the bread and the wine into the inner reality of the body and blood of Christ... this happens in a way surpassing understanding, by the power of the Holy Spirit. 'The visible elements, the forms of bread and wine, become the 'blessed sacrament' of the invisible and mysterious presence of the risen and glorified Lord. This presence can be grasped only by faith, not by our senses' (paras 50, 51).[1]

Readers seeking further knowledge and appreciation of this central belief of the Catholic Church are recommended to read the clear presentation found in 'One Bread One Body' referred to in the Bibliography.

> 'The Sacrament of the Altar is always at the heart of the Church's life, and the life of every dedicated Catholic. The Church's very history bears witness to this' (para 6).[2]

Throughout history, from the stories of the Roman martyrs to the persecuted Catholic heroes of Elizabethan England – and in modern times the hounded Catholics of Communist China – the need to celebrate and communicate at Mass has been more important than life itself. This is well illustrated in the life and courageous spirituality of Margaret Clitherow, the heroic butcher's wife of York, who endangered her life to make the Eucharist available to family and friends.

Martyr of the Eucharist

ST MARGARET CLITHEROW (c.1556-1586)

Almost in the centre of the city of York, you can wander down a short street of tudor-style houses called 'The Shambles'. The Tudor houses there may have been artificially maintained, but it was here, in this street, in the 1580s, that the Clitherow family lived, above the butcher's shop on the ground floor. John, a wealthy butcher, married Margaret Middleton, daughter of the Sheriff of York in 1571; they were a highly respected couple in the city. As time passed they had three children, Henry, William and Anne. About three years into their marriage Margaret gave up the new religion of Queen Elizabeth I and became a Catholic, while husband John remained a member of the Anglican Church.

In 1581 an Act of the Queen's Council was passed 'To retain Her Majesty's subjects in due obedience'. It declared that it was high treason to reconcile anyone or to be reconciled to the Catholic Church and imposed a new scale of heavy fines on anyone who did not, each Sunday, attend the Anglican church service. It became a capital offence to harbour or give hospitality to a priest.

Evelyn Waugh writes of this in his *Edmund Campion* (the Jesuit intellectual and priest on the run, who was tortured and hung, drawn and quartered at Tyburn, London on 1 December 1581):

> 'The object of this legislation was to outlaw and ruin the Catholic community. It will be seen that under the new code a family of four adults who elected to lead a regular Catholic life, attending Mass and eschewing the Protestant services, were liable, if they were fortunate enough to keep out of prison, to a total yearly payment of over £15,500 (or in modern currency about £930,000). There was scarcely a family in the country capable of sustaining an imposition of this size, nor in fact, was any obliged to do so, for Masses were said in secret, the vessels kept behind sliding panels, and the priests smuggled in and out of doors through concealed passages. But there was still the non-attendance at Protestant services. In the final analysis, none but the wealthiest had any choice between submission and destitution.[3]

Almost immediately after her conversion Margaret began to secretly harbour priests, who celebrated the Eucharist in her home for Catholic neighbours and friends. Margaret, undeterred by the penalty of life imprisonment for doing so (only repealed in 1798), was determined to educate her children in the Catholic Faith. With the help of visiting priests, she did so, using secret means, like the two **Recusant** catechetical songs in Appendix Five. In the following years

Margaret hid many priests, some of whom were caught, in other places, and executed. Acting on a tip-off, on 10 March 1586, the pursuivants (Queen Elizabeth I's agents), raided the Clitherow house and discovered, in a secret cupboard, sacred vessels and vestments for the celebration of Mass. Margaret was arrested; she was arraigned, on 14th March, at the York Assizes, charged with harbouring priests and attending Mass. She refused to plead guilty or not guilty, because she did not want her children brought to court and forced to give witness against her; as the pursuivants threatened. The penalty was to be crushed to death. On Lady Day, 1586, the penalty was carried out at the toll booth on Ousebridge. Margaret was popular in the city and the regular executioners had fled the town; four beggars had to be bribed to carry out the sentence. Bare footed, in a simple white shift, Margaret was staked out, with a sharp stone under her back and a heavy door was placed over her; weights were piled on top until she died. Her final words were 'Jesu! Jesu! Jesu! Have mercy on me'.

Margaret's two sons, Henry and William became priests to continue the work of their mother, and their sister Anne, became a nun. She was declared a martyr of the Catholic Faith in 1970, along with 39 other English men and women, who died in Elizabethan times trying to provide the persecuted Catholic community in England and Wales with the Eucharist. The Forty Martyrs were only a small selection of the many hundreds who at that time, and throughout the centuries, willingly gave their lives to attend or provide the Mass for their fellow Catholics.

SUMMARY

The altar is the most important and central feature of every Catholic church. It is the symbol of the unity (the communion) of the community that gathers there; it is accorded dignity because it is the consecrated table of the Eucharist, both sacrifice and sacrament. The Eucharistic life of the baptised People of God (the local Church) is paramount. As Pope Benedict XVI writes, 'the Sacrament of the Altar is always at the heart of the Church's life'.[3]

NOTES – CHAPTER 3

1. *'One Bread, One Body'* by the Bishops of England and Wales, pp.33 and 34.
2. *'Sacramentum Caritatis'* by Pope Benedict XVI, p.11.
3. *'Edmund Campion'* by Evelyn Waugh, p.88.

CHAPTER 4 — *Focus:* THE AMBO

THE WORD OF GOD

The Ambo

In the **sanctuary** of a modern Catholic church, close to the altar, can be seen the ambo, from which the Scriptures are proclaimed. While the reading and reflection upon the Word of God has always, from the earliest days, been an essential part of the community's celebration of the Eucharist, there has not always been a special place allotted to it. In the homes of the first Christians, and in the Church of the Catacombs, there was no room for such and it was not until the time of the Emperor Constantine that wooden structures were provided, in order to raise the reader above the level of the standing congregation. These special stands gradually became more substantial and great dignity was given to the ambo, and so to the Scriptures, when beautifully decorated stonework became the norm.

Advent of pulpits

As time passed, in the late Middle Ages, due to the dedication of the Franciscan and Dominican preachers, sermons became divorced from an exposition of the Scripture readings and ambos were replaced by pulpits. Some of these, especially in response to the emphasis put upon preaching by the Protestant reformers, became both very ornate and elevated high above the lay congregation. These pulpits were dispensed with by the Second Vatican Council, in the mid-60s, and the simpler ambo, from which the Word of God was to be proclaimed and expounded upon, was restored.

Altar and Ambo

On the relationship between the altar and the ambo, the Council has this to say:

> 'The Church has always venerated the divine Scriptures just as she venerates the body of the Lord, since from the table of both the word of God and of the body of Christ she unceasingly receives and offers to the people the bread of life, especially in the sacred liturgy' (para 6).[1]

This teaching has been repeated and amplified, over the years, in a range of official documents; for example, in *One Bread One Body* by the Catholic Bishops' Conference of England and Wales:

> 'As Christians we find our nourishment and strength in the Scriptures precisely because God speaks to us now through them. Word and Sacrament are a seamless robe. Scripture and Eucharist are intimately interwoven in the life of the Church' (para 23).[2]

From *The Gift of Scripture:*

> 'We are fed by the sacrament, but also by the word. We are invited to 'take and eat,' to 'take and drink', but also to 'take and read' (para 4).[3]

And more recently, from Pope Benedict XVI's *Sacramentum Caritatis*:

> 'The liturgy of the word and the Eucharistic liturgy… are so closely interconnected that they form but one single act of worship. There is an intrinsic bond between the word of God and the Eucharist' (para 44).[4]

The ambo is then of equal importance to the altar, although here we have, for historical reasons, focused first on the altar. The average Catholic is exposed regularly to Christ, present in his word, during the weekly celebration of the Lord's Day.

> 'It is above all through the liturgy that Christians come into contact with scripture... Christ is present in his word, because it is he himself who speaks when sacred scripture is read in the Church. Written text thus becomes living word' (para 27).[5]

Impact of the Proclaimed Word

The best illustration of these words from the Vatican's Biblical Commission is the story told by St Athanasius in his *Life of St Antony*.[6]

> 'Not six months after the death of his parents, Antony went according to his custom to the Lord's house... He entered the church, and it happened that the Gospel was being read, and he heard the Lord saying to the rich man, "If you would be perfect, go, sell what you possess and give to the poor, and you will have treasure in heaven" (Mt 19:21) Antony, ...as if the passage had been read on his account, went out immediately from the church, and gave the possessions of his forefathers to the villagers... All the rest that was moveable he sold, and having got together much money he gave it to the poor, reserving a little however, for his sister's sake... And again he went into the church, and he heard the Lord say in the Gospel, "Do not be anxious about your life" (Mt 6:25). He could stay no longer, but went out and gave those things also to the poor... he henceforth devoted himself outside his house to discipline.' (Written about 360 AD.)

Few stories from the early centuries of Christianity circulated as widely and rapidly as Athanasius' telling of the life of St Antony, the fourth-century hermit of the Egyptian desert. The book motivated countless Christians to take up the contemplative life in seclusion (see Glossary: **Desert Fathers**). And all this came about through hearing the Scriptures read, from the ambo, in church.

Revised Lectionary

On a Sunday, the liturgy of the word, which takes place at the ambo, consists of four passages from Scripture. The selection of texts from the **Bible** is arranged, for Sundays (there is a different arrangement for Masses during the week), on a three-year cycle, so that as much of the Bible as possible is covered. This was one of the most important changes made by the Second Vatican Council. Scott Hahn explains this transformation in his *Letter and Spirit*.[7]

> The most significant change came about in 1969, with the introduction of the revised lectionary… there can be no doubt that it was a major development in the life of the Church. The lectionary was designed specifically for the purpose of highlighting the essential relationship between scripture and liturgy. The old lectionary had covered a one-year cycle; the new book covered three years. The old lectionary's Sunday readings had been chosen almost exclusively from the gospels and epistles; the new lectionary employed most of the content of most of the books of the Bible, both Old and New Testaments… the three-year lectionary was an ecumenical event. Within a year, the Presbyterian churches imitated it, and Anglican and Lutheran bodies soon adopted it as well. This, in itself, is a remarkable development.

There is a theme to the selection of readings given for each Sunday, and major feast days of the year, according to the Season. At least the first reading from the Old Testament and the third reading, which is always from a Gospel, fit the theme. Between the first and second reading, one of the psalms from the Book of Psalms is sung or read. Lay readers usually read the first two extracts from the Bible (and the psalm should be sung) but the Gospel passage is always read by a deacon or priest; and out of respect for the words of the Gospel, the people stand to hear it.

The Homily

The reading of the Gospel is followed by a homily delivered by the celebrant; this is not a sermon, but an interpretation and exposition of the Bible readings. This too was restored by the Second Vatican Council;

> 'The treasures of the Bible are to be opened up more lavishly, so that richer fare may be provided for the faithful at the table of God's Word ... by means of the homily the mysteries of the faith and the guiding principles of the Christian life are expounded from the sacred text during the course of the liturgical year. The homily, therefore, is to be highly esteemed as part of the liturgy itself' (paras 51, 52).[8]

The prominence and dignity of the ambo in the church, and the above quotations from the official documents, demonstrate how central the Word of God is to Catholic Spirituality.

Scripture proclaimed

In the Book of Nehemiah it tells how the Jewish People, on their return from Exile in Babylon, re-built the walls of

Jerusalem. When the walls were completed 'and the Israelites had settled in their towns, all the people assembled' (ch 8:1); the scribe, Ezra, 'read the Law aloud from daybreak till noon... and all the people listened attentively to the Book of the Law' (v 2-3). Apart from the remarkable stamina and interest of the assembled crowd, the event highlights the point that the ordinary people could not read and there was just the one copy of the Book of the Law. Throughout most of Christian history the situation has been the same; the ordinary churchgoers could not read and copies of the Bible were rare and precious, having been copied individually by the **Benedictine** monks. The thousands of monasteries, throughout the British Isles and the whole of Europe, had copies of the Scriptures in their libraries and the educated clergy had access, but most parish churches would only have the one copy. While the possession of a personal copy of the whole Bible (in the late Middle Ages the wealthy could acquire the Book of Psalms or one of the Gospels) became possible after the invention of printing in 1440, most Christians only heard the Word of God when it was read to them at Sunday Mass.

Lectio Divina

This did not prevent the Christian hermits of the fourth and fifth centuries, known as the **Desert Fathers** having and meditating upon individual Books, or parts of a Book, of the Bible. They pioneered the private, meditative use of Scripture; where it was possible. It was the Carthusian monk, Guigo II (who died around 1188) who led a discussion on the correct way to read the Bible, for the development of one's personal spiritual life. According to Guigo there are four stages that can be discerned and followed in the reading of a Biblical text and its use as a prompt to meditation:

1. reading *(lectio)*
2. meditation *(meditatio)*
3. prayer *(oratio)*
4. contemplation *(contemplatio)*.

Guigo proposes that we read the text slowly, aware that here is God's word and the Holy Spirit desires to communicate to us through these words. (In the Eastern Churches people call the Bible "God's love letter to his people".) 'We read it carefully, looking for the story or the meaning of the passage. It is helpful to look out for details, to keep an eye on the verbs, which tell us who is acting, or what is happening. Silence is important, as it can take time for us to see the details'[9] (quotation from *With the Word of God* one of the recent books that is making *Lectio Divina* popular again). The reading, Guigo says, leads on to a meditation on what we find – not in the sense of emptying our minds of everything, but rather allowing our minds to focus and concentrate upon the meaning and imagery of the text, with all external thoughts excluded. This activity leads naturally to prayer, as the only appropriate response to what we have encountered. This leads us, finally, into a quiet entrance into and awareness of the presence of God in contemplation. In a few terse lines Guigo sets out the relationship between the four activities:

> 'Reading without meditation is sterile.
> Meditation without reading is prone to error.
> Prayer without meditation is lukewarm.
> Meditation without prayer is barren.
> Prayer with devotion achieves contemplation.'

Guigo's scheme was widely accepted and followed in the Middle Ages – and is currently popular again – because it unlocked the devotional riches of Scripture. For example, one of the greatest masters of prayer in the Middle Ages, and founder of *Devotio Moderna,* Geert Zerbolt van

Zutphen (1367-1400) endorsed it fully in his books and offers a definition of meditation, which was a good synthesis of medieval thought.

The Ignatian Model

A related approach is associated with St Ignatius of Loyola (c1491-1556) and his followers. Loyola – the founder of the Society of Jesus, usually known as 'The Jesuits' – developed a technique of imaginative engagement, in which the reader of the Scripture text imagines his or herself to be projected into the Biblical narrative, viewing and experiencing it from within. This is accompanied with a prayerful engagement with the text (in a similar fashion to *Lection Divina*) in order that the text really impacts upon the reader. St Ignatius sets out the basic principles of his method in his 'First Exercise' (see below), considering how the reader of a gospel passage relating to Jesus should approach the text.

> 'The first preamble is to form a visual conception of the place. It should be noted at this point when the contemplation is on something that is visible (such as contemplating Christ our Lord during his life on earth), the image will consist of seeing with the mind's eye the physical place where the object we wish to contemplate is present. By the physical place I mean, for instance, a temple or mountain where Jesus or the Blessed Virgin is to be found, depending on the subject of the contemplation. In meditations on something that is invisible, as here in meditation on sins, the mental image will be imagined, by considering my soul imprisoned in its corruptible body, and my entire being in this valley as an exile among wild animals. By "entire being" I mean body and soul.

The second is to ask God, our Lord, for what I want and desire. The request must be according to the subject matter. Therefore, if the contemplation is on the resurrection, I shall ask for joy with Christ rejoicing; if it is on the passion, I shall ask for pain, tears and suffering with Christ suffering.'[10]

The above is from Loyola's *Spiritual Exercises* and modern readers, in reading such texts, should bear in mind the cultural thought patterns, concepts and language of the period in which they were written.

The Spiritual Exercises

The *Spiritual Exercises* is one of the most influential Catholic books ever written. In many languages it has been published some 4,500 times and the estimated number of copies printed is 4.5 million. The purpose of the book is established in its opening paragraph: 'preparing and disposing our soul to rid itself of all its disordered affections and then, after their removal, of seeking and finding God's will in the ordering of our life for the salvation of our soul'.

It was not only the life of St Antony, the desert hermit, whose life was changed by hearing Scripture read at the Eucharist. Augustine of Hippo was brought back to the faith of his childhood by first reading a Scripture passage and, following that, hearing the homilies on Scripture of Ambrose, the saintly bishop of Milan.

The Restless Flame

ST AUGUSTINE OF HIPPO (354–430)

Louis de Wohl, a Catholic novelist, once famous for his historical novels, wove the life of Augustine of Hippo into a best-selling book. He perceptively called the novel *The*

Restless Flame, and then demonstrated how apt was that title for one of the greatest Christian minds of history. Augustine's own famous and influential book in the development of Catholic Spirituality is *The Confessions of St Augustine*. It was written some thirteen years after Augustine's conversion and baptism, about the year 400 AD. Born in Algeria of a pagan father and a Christian mother, Augustine lost his faith in adolescence; took a concubine at 17 and had a son by her. A brilliant rhetorician, he was led away from his mother's faith and became caught up, for many years, in the heresy of Manichaeism. Augustine was a very gifted philosopher and teacher, who had a glittering career in the Empire ahead of him. It was for career advancement that he left the mother of his child and became betrothed to a 12-year-old heiress. After months of turmoil, and endless debate, he rejected Manichaeism and came under the influence of the greatest Christian preacher of that time, Ambrose, bishop of Milan. In Book 8, chapter 12, of his *Confessions* Augustine tells the story of the moment when he was finally, after many years of struggle, converted. It came through reading the Bible.

He records how one day he was tormented, praying and yet not praying, trying to reason his way out of the mess his life was in. He wandered into the garden of the house where he, and his friend Alypius lodged, then 'I heard the voice of a boy, or a girl, I don't know which, coming from a neighbour's garden. S/he was chanting, over and over again, "Tolle lege. Tolle lege, Tolle lege" ("Take up and read"). Immediately I started to think, whether it was usual for children, in some game or other, to sing out such words; I could never remember the like before. So holding back my tears, that wanted to flow, I interpreted what I heard as a command to me from Heaven to open the book, and read the first passage that caught my eye. I had heard how the hermit, Antony, doing the same, came upon the passage "Go and sell what you have and give to the poor and you shall have treasure in heaven, and come follow me". Those words marked the moment of Anthony's conversion. So I quickly return to where Alypius was sitting, for I had left my copy of the Scriptures with him. I opened the book (at Romans 13:13) and in silence read the paragraph on which my eyes first fell, 'Let us live decently, as in the light of day; with no orgies or drunkenness, no promiscuity or licentiousness, and no wrangling or jealousy. Let your armour be the Lord Jesus Christ, and stop worrying about how your disordered natural inclinations may be fulfilled." Augustine concludes, "I read no further, I did not need to, for instantly, as the sentence ended – by a light, as it were, of security filled and infused my heart – all the gloom of doubt vanished away".[11] He went on to become Bishop of Hippo, Doctor of the Church, and one of the greatest and most influential theologians in Christian history.

This St Augustine of Hippo (354-430) should not be confused with St Augustine of Canterbury, (d.604), a Benedictine monk sent by Pope Gregory the Great to re-found the Church in England; and he became the first Archbishop of Canterbury.

SUMMARY

Although there has not always been an ambo, standing in the sanctuary, close to the altar, the Scriptures have always been read at the celebration of the Eucharist. The restoration of the ambo for the public proclamation of God's word, and the homily expounding it, were important reforms of the Second Vatican Council. The ambo is accorded equal dignity with the altar, for at the altar the Body of Christ is broken and shared, while at the ambo the Word of God is proclaimed and broken open for all to share. As the Bishops of England and Wales have said, 'We are fed by the sacrament, but also by the word. We are invited to 'take and eat', but also to 'take and read'.[12]

Lectio Divina and the Ignatian method are ways designed to help Christians to 'take and read' and to use Scripture as a springboard and inspiration for a deeper relationship with God, through prayer and contemplation.

NOTES – CHAPTER 4

1. The Second Vatican Council's Constitution on Revelation, p.125.
2. *One Bread One Body* by the Bishops of England and Wales, p.19.
3. *The Gift of Scripture* by the Bishops of England and Wales, p.16.
4. *Sacramentum Caritatis* by Pope Benedict XVI, p.44.
5. *The Interpretation of Scripture* by the Pontifical Biblical Commission, quoted in *The Gift of Scripture*, p.53.
6. *Life of St Antony* by St Athanasius, quoted in the novel *The Restless Flame,* by Louis de Wohl, p.2.
7. *Letter and Spirit* by Scott Hahn, pp.2,3.
8. The Second Vatican Council's Constitution on the Liturgy, p.155.
9. *With the Word of God* by Sister Jude Groden RSM, p.9.
10. *Spiritual Exercises of St Ignatius* by Geroge E, Ganss, SJ, p.67.
11. *The Confessions of St Augustine* by St Augustine of Hippo, quoted in the novel *The Restless Flame,* by Louis de Wohl.
12. *The Gift of Scripture* by the Bishops of England and Wales, p.11.

CHAPTER 5   *Focus:* ROLE OF SCRIPTURE

THE WITNESS OF SCRIPTURE

Scripture essential

An ignorance of Holy Scripture is a huge handicap to anyone who seeks to explore Christian Spirituality and develop his or her own spiritual life. Knowledge of Christ, and growth in discipleship, is only possible through a familiarity with the Word of God. Jesus himself pointed out, after his Resurrection (Lk 24:27 and 24:45) that he could not be understood apart from a knowledge of Moses and the Prophets. Pope Benedict XVI makes this point in *Jesus of Nazareth*.

> 'In his discourses after the Resurrection, Jesus insists that he can be understood only in the context of "the Law and the Prophets" and that his community can live only in this properly understood context.'[1]

The Apostle Philip understood this when he told Nathaniel, 'we have found the one Moses wrote about in the Law, and about whom the prophets also wrote – Jesus of Nazareth, the son of Joseph' (Jn 1:44) To which Nathaniel made his famous retort, 'Nazareth! Can anything good come from there!' (He was, in time, of course, forced to eat his words!) Later on in his ministry Jesus himself confirmed that his mission was to fulfil the Law and the Prophets; 'Do not think that I have come to abolish the Law or the Prophets; I have not come to abolish them but to fulfil them' (Mt 5:17).

Inspired Word of God

But how to read and benefit from Scripture? First it has to be said that in Christian/Catholic theology the terms 'Bible' and 'Scripture' are equivalent in meaning; as are 'biblical' and 'scriptural'. It is next important to appreciate that, for the Christian, Scripture is respected and revered as the inspired Word of God. As the Bishops of England and Wales make clear in their booklet *The Gift of Scripture* 'God is the author of Scripture, but the sacred authors are also true authors'. Lucidly and simply, it explains how Scripture is inspired by the Holy Spirit, who used human, time-bound, authors.

> 'God communicates with us out of love, and in so doing adapts the word to our human situation… The Scriptures themselves proclaim that they are inspired by God, that God is their author, and that they were written by the inspiration of the Holy Spirit. Inspiration should be seen as an extraordinary action of the Holy Spirit in the mind and heart of those involved in the production of the Scriptures.
>
> Ultimately, the inspiration of Scripture remains a mystery of God's loving outreach to us, a mystery which we cannot fully fathom.'[2]

Catholic understanding of Scripture, Pope John Paul II says, "does not focus attention only on the human aspects of biblical revelation, which is sometimes the mistake of the historical-critical method, nor only on the divine aspects, as fundamentalism would have it; it strives to highlight both of them, united as they are in the divine 'condescension' which is the foundation of all Scripture".[3]

God reveals

St Paul tells us that 'long ago God spoke to our ancestors in many and varied ways by the prophets, but in these last days God has spoken to us by his Son' (Heb 1:1-2).

This communication, which we call 'divine revelation', in and through which God reveals a little, a very little, of himself, is in order to build a relationship with humankind. The Second Vatican Council document says:

> 'The invisible God, out of the abundance of his love, addresses people as friends and converses with them, to invite them to communion with him and to receive them into that communion' (para 2).[4]

Love always seeks union. John in his first letter (4:12) tells us that God is love, who seeks union with those he loves.

> 'No-one has ever seen God; but if we love one another, God lives in us and his love is made complete in us'. And 'whoever lives in love lives in God, and God lives in him' (v.16).

The Three Loves

Jesus did not invent the commandment to 'love the Lord your God with all your heart and with all your soul and with all your strength and with all your mind'; and 'love your neighbour as yourself'. The first is a quotation from the Book of Deuteronomy 6:4 and the second text is found in Leviticus 19:18. These quotations are from what Judaism calls 'The Books of Moses', because they were traditionally believed to have been written by Moses; however this has not, universally, been accepted by Biblical scholars for some time. The quotation from Deuteronomy opens with the words, 'Hear, O Israel: The Lord our God, the Lord is one' and the whole passage forms the prayer, and primal confession of belief, of the Jewish People; it is known as the *Shema*, and is used in all public and private prayer. Jesus broadened the Shema by adding the words from Leviticus; making it a threefold love; a total, whole-person, love of God, matched by love of neighbour and love of self. This threefold love is the bedrock and foundation stone of Christian Spirituality. Just as a three-legged stool will not work, if one of the legs is missing, so too there can be no authentic Spirituality with the descriptive adjective 'Christian' or 'Catholic' without a balance between the three loves.

Encountering God's Love

Pope Benedict XVI wrote these opening words to his first letter to the world,

> "God is love, and he who abides in love abides in God, and God abides in him" (1 Jn 4:16). These words express with remarkable clarity the heart of the Christian faith: the Christian image of God and the resulting image of humankind and its destiny. In the same verse St John also offers a kind of summary of the Christian life: "We have come to know and to believe in the love God has for us". *We have come to believe in God's love:* in these words the Christian can express the fundamental decision of his life. Being Christian is not the result of an ethical choice or a lofty idea, but the encounter with an event, a person, which gives life a new horizon and a decisive direction'.[5]

Thus Pope Benedict makes clear what Christian Spirituality is; it is the encounter with the person of Jesus Christ, which gives life a new horizon and direction. For 'Christ wants to draw all of us into his humanity and so into his Sonship, into his total belonging to God.'

St Paul's use of an early Christian prayer, in his letter to the Christians of Ephesus, seems appropriate as a summary of the above.

Grounded in love

'I pray that, according to the riches of his glory, he may grant that you may be strengthened in your inner being with power through his Spirit, and that Christ may dwell in your hearts through faith, as you are being rooted and grounded in love. I pray that you may have the power to comprehend, with all the saints, what is the breadth and length and height and depth, and to know the love of Christ that surpasses knowledge, so that you may be filled with all the fullness of God' (Eph 3:16-19).

An Introduction to the Bible

Approaching the Bible seriously for the first time, with a great desire to learn and benefit from the reading, the newcomer is likely to forget that the Bible is not a book like any other. It is rather a collection of Books; a 'library' containing many different types of literature. So there is 'The Book of Genesis', 'The Book of Leviticus', 'The Book of Psalms', 'The Book of Job' etc. Each of those is a different genre of writing, each written by different authors, with a different intention in writing. What we know as the Old Testament (or Hebrew Bible) gradually came together over a period of a thousand years. What the dedicated newcomer must *not* do is start at the beginning of Genesis and set out to read all the way through to the Book of Revelation. The Bible was never intended to be approached that way. It should be recalled that until modern times most Christians could not read or write; and this was even more true of most of the Jewish People of Old Testament times. Although most of the Bible was written for public proclamation, not private reading, it is the inspired Word of God and the best possible source of nurturing the spiritual life. Wilfrid Harrington OP has proposed the following introduction to the Old Testament:

1. Start with *Tobit:* This is found in Catholic Bibles but not in Protestant ones, as it is a Deutero-canonical book (see below). A surprisingly modern tale – a true novelette. Notice how skilfully the stories of Tobit and of Sarah are blended in chapter 3. And the book closes in the familiar 'they lived happily ever after' fashion.

2. *2 Samuel 11-12:* The moving story of the sin and repentance of David. The whole of 2 Samuel is remarkably vivid – the finest piece of narrative writing in the Old Testament.

3. *Genesis 42-45:* The reunion of Joseph with his family in Egypt. Notice how Joseph declares that God had directed the whole affair.

4. *Hosea 6 and 11:* So much for that touchy, stern, vengeful God of the Old Testament!

5. *Jeremiah 20:7-18:* A prophet's cry from the heart.

   Ch 31: The same prophet's words of comfort to a shattered people.

6. *Song of Songs 4-5:* The ecstasy of love. True love of man and woman is a gift of God.

7. *Job 38:1 to 40:5:* With splendid irony the Lord questions Job. He did not have an answer to his personal problem – what does he know of all the works of God? Man stands before his Creator.[6]

New Testament Background

The first, and earliest, part of the New Testament to be written is the first letter that St Paul wrote to the Christian community of the bustling seaport city of Thessalonica. It is generally accepted that it was written in the year 51 AD; so some twenty years after the death and resurrection of

Christ. The second letter was probably written about six months later. It is instructive to realise that for over that period of twenty years the Christian communities had met weekly for the Eucharist (see 1 Cor 11:17-34 where St Paul reprimands the community for not conducting it properly) with no Gospels or Christian literature to draw upon. In those community gatherings, on the Lord's Day, the teaching and understanding of the Gospel message developed *before* anyone put pen to paper. The Christian community, the Church, therefore came into being long before the writings we now call the New Testament.

The Gospels

The last part of the New Testament to be written was probably (scholars debate and argue over the precise date) the Gospel of John, in 95. Its style and content is very different from the other gospels; which are grouped together and called 'the **Synoptic Gospels**'. The first Gospel to be written, in about 64 AD, probably in Rome, was by Mark, who, it is believed, was the secretary of St Peter. (Some have said that Mark's Gospel reflects the preaching and teaching of Peter). It is the shortest Gospel and not so structured as the others. It takes only about fifty minutes to read from beginning to end. The reader is advised not to start with the Gospel of John, but with Mark's and then to turn to Paul's two letters to the Thessalonians, to get a 'feel' for life in those early Christian communities.

It is difficult to imagine what would have happened to the inspired word of God, the Bible, if one scholar had not settled down to translate it from Hebrew (the Old Testament) and the Greek (New Testament) into the common language of his time, which was Latin. St Jerome was that scholar and modern Christians owe him a great debt of gratitude.

The Lion of the Bible

ST JEROME (c.345–420)

The legend of the lion, that appears in paintings, at the feet of Eusebius Hieronymus Sophronius (better known to modern readers as St Jerome) is fairly well known. According to the story, while Jerome was living in Bethlehem, about the year 410, he was working one day, with three assistants, on his translation of the Bible, when a lion appeared at the door of the room. The three assistants took off as fast as they could through a side door and out of a window! Jerome carried on intently with his work.

The lion approached him, the story goes, and held up a front paw. Jerome took it in his hand and saw immediately that it was swollen and enflamed. He searched and found that a large thorn had pierced the paw and had been broken off, presumably by earlier efforts of the lion to help himself. Jerome extracted the thorn and bathed the wound. The lion curled up at his feet; and the story goes, continued, ever after, to live peaceably nearby.

Whether there is any element of truth in the legend or not, what is well established is that St Jerome was one of the greatest intellects, with one of the most versatile minds, of antiquity. During his restless life he travelled the entire Roman Empire making many friends, and experimenting with different forms of the monastic and hermit life in different places. He became secretary to Pope Damasus I and produced copious books, letters, etc., defending the Church against a range of heresies.

Pictures usually include the painting of a cardinal's hat; it being assumed that Damasus had made him a cardinal, but there is no evidence of that being the case. Most of all he was an erudite Catholic scholar, who mastered the legacies of the Latin, Greek and Biblical literature and he taught the importance of educated people reading the Bible in the original languages. However his most lasting contribution to spirituality was his Latin translation of almost the entire Bible. This translation is called 'The Vulgate' because it was written in the 'vulgar' (Latin for 'common') language of the people. It had been Jerome's plan and intention to make the Bible, written in Hebrew and Greek – languages unknown to ordinary people – available to everyone in their own tongue.

SUMMARY

Scripture is so important to the development of the spiritual life of the Catholic that the above two chapters have been dedicated to it. St Paul, writing in his second letter to Timothy explains perfectly the role and purpose of scripture:

> 'All scripture is inspired by God and can profitably be used for teaching, refuting error, for guiding people's lives and teaching them to be holy. This is how someone who is dedicated to God becomes fully equipped and ready for any good work' (2 Tim 3:16).

NOTES – CHAPTER 5

1. *Jesus of Nazareth* by Pope Benedict XVI, p.121.
2. *The Gift of Scripture* by the Bishops of England and Wales, p.17.
3. *De Tout Coeur* by Pope John Paul II, quoted in *The Gift of Scripture*, p.22.
4. The Second Vatican Council's Constitution on Revelation, p.112.
5. *Deus Caritas Est;* the first Encylical Letter of Pope Benedict XVI, p.3.
6. Precise source unkown.

CHAPTER 6 — *Focus:* CELEBRANT'S CHAIR

AUTHORITY AND GUIDANCE

East-facing churches

If you were ever to be lost, seeking your bearings, in an old cathedral city, like Durham or Canterbury, or perhaps, an English country town or village, you only have to check the direction that the cathedral or pre-Reformation parish church is facing. All churches built in England and Wales before the Reformation face East; (the building being constructed in a line, East to West, with the sanctuary at the east end). These buildings look to Jerusalem and the site of Christ's death and resurrection. In the period of Christian history (100-313), often call 'The Age of the Domestic Church' because most services took place in the home, there was no concern about the direction faced; this only happened post-313, when churches started to be built.

Presider's chair

Prominent in these early buildings was the altar, and behind it the presider or celebrant's chair. Normally in those early years the presider, or celebrant, would be the bishop. His special chair, or throne, was called the **cathedra** and was an important symbol of his unifying and teaching role. With the passing of time, and the vast increase in the numbers of Christians, the bishop had to delegate his priests to represent him, but the celebrant's chair remained an important symbol of the leading and teaching role of the bishop's representative.

However, as time passed, as we have seen, the altar did

not remain where the people could gather round it, but 'during the eighth century, the altar was pushed farther into the apse until it ended up against the back wall. In this position, the back of the altar began to be embellished. Eventually, more emphasis was placed on the back embellishment, called the reredos, than on the altar table itself.'[1] One of the consequences of this was that the presider's chair was either abandoned completely or, in cathedrals, placed to one side.

Teaching with authority

Matthew writes in his Gospel, how Jesus on 'seeing the crowds, went onto the mountainside. And when he was seated his disciples came to him. Then he began to speak' (5:1-2). Jesus, in doing this, is following the traditional practice of the rabbi, or teacher, sitting down to teach and his disciples and listeners gathering at his feet to listen and learn. Mark appears to be speaking of the same occasion when he writes, 'Jesus now went up onto the mountain and summoned those he wanted. So they came to him and he appointed twelve; they were to be his companions and to be sent out to proclaim his message' (3:13-14). It is clear from both of these passages that Jesus is the Master, who teaches with authority. This is the Scriptural background to the *cathedra* or presider's chair in the church. It is the Master who calls the Twelve Apostles and later, when there are eleven, he gives them authority to go out and preach the Good News. This is crystal clear in the final command of Christ to his Apostles:

> 'All authority in heaven and earth has been given to me. Go, therefore, make disciples of all nations; baptise them in the name of the Father and of the Son and of the Holy Spirit, and teach them to observe all the commands I gave you. And look, I am with

you always; yes, to the end of time' (the final words of Matthew's Gospel 28:19-20).

The role of the Apostles

Those magnificent words addressed to the Apostles – there is no one else present – empowers them and places on their shoulders responsibility for the mission of the Church. Christ will be the Head of the Church, always present until the end of time, but authority is given to the Apostles to lead the visible community of Christ. The Church is 'apostolic', founded, by Christ's express command, on the Twelve. Paul in Ephesians, and elsewhere, emphasises how all authority resides with the Risen Christ, 'God has put all things under his feet and made him, as he is above all things, the head of the Church; which is his Body, the fullness of him who is filled, all in all' (1:22-23).

While they were alive the Apostles presided over the communities and their worship, but the spread of the Church necessitated the authorisation of 'elders', (of these the terms 'presbyter' and 'episcopos' are used and appear to be interchangeable) who took over the presiding role. It is these, the Orthodox churches, the Anglican Communion and the Catholic Church believe became the 'bishops', who carry forward the responsibility and teaching role bestowed by Christ on the Apostles.

This Catholic teaching is expressed by the Second Vatican Council:

> 'The bishops have been appointed by the Holy Spirit, and as successors of the apostles as pastors of souls. Together with the Supreme Pontiff and under his authority, they have been sent to continue throughout the ages the work of Christ, the supreme pastor' (para 2).[2]

Symbol of teaching authority

In each Catholic church the celebrant's chair is symbolically important, because it is the 'cathedra' for that community. It is, by rights, the **Diocesan** bishop's chair, but just as the Apostles had to delegate their authority to elders, so too the modern bishop, delegates his authority and role, in a particular community, to the authorised priest. When the bishop visits the parish community it is his chair to use; at all other times it is the chair of the celebrating priest. No one else, deacon or pastoral lay assistant, should make use of it.

Authoritative guidance

The bishops of the Church, with the Bishop of Rome, the Pope, have responsibility to ensure that Christ's message and Good News is passed on accurately and without error or blemish. This authoritative guidance has been necessary over the period of nearly 2,000 years since Christ laid that charge on his apostles and their successors. Erroneous thinking and teachings have assailed the Church from the earliest days. Through meeting together in the Councils of the Church (from the First Council of Nicaea in 325 to the Second Vatican Council, 1962-1965) the Bishop of Rome, with the Bishops, have dealt with many erroneous teachings, or heresies, that have been examined in the light of Scripture and Tradition, debated and, where necessary, condemned. (A few of those, which have a bearing upon Spirituality today are noted in Appendix Two.

Early spiritual guides

Naturally, teaching on doctrine and morals is closely related to teaching on spirituality and all matters that have a bearing on an individual's spiritual life. An inspection of

Appendix One reveals that most of the spiritual guides of the first seven centuries were bishops. Only when the Religious Orders, from the twelfth century onwards, became dominate in Europe, do they provide outstanding spiritual writers and guides. Each Religious Order has its own charism, that is, its own particular, inspired gift, and direction which illuminates how best a person might develop their spiritual life and pursue holiness. For example, the Franciscan Order, following the example of their founder, St Francis of Assisi, puts their emphasis upon detachment from material possessions; while the more recent Passionists focus upon the love of Christ exhibited in his Passion and Death.

The humble minister

The presider at the Eucharist is also the celebrant or minister. The word 'minister' is originally derived from the Latin word, '*manus*', for 'hand'; so in Christ's time 'minister' was the Latin word for 'servant'; someone who was 'on hand' and 'gave a hand'. (And probably got cuffed round the head with a hand!) Jesus acted as a humble servant or minister when he knelt at the feet of each of his Apostles, at the Last Supper, and with his own hands washed their feet. He concluded his action with this instruction to his friends, 'Do you understand what I have done to you? You call me Master and Lord, and rightly; so I am. If I, then, the Lord and Master, have washed your feet, you must wash each other's feet. I have given you an example so that you may copy what I have done to you' (Jn 13:12-14).

Importance of Maundy Thursday

At the evening Eucharistic celebration on Holy Thursday (traditionally, in England, called **Maundy Thursday**) the day before Good Friday, the celebrant leaves his chair, takes off his outer vestment, ties an apron around his waist and, in imitation of Christ Jesus, kneels and washes the feet of twelve people from the congregation. This takes place in every Catholic church in the world and, in Rome, the Pope personally conducts the same service with twelve poor people. The Church likes to keep this lesson that Jesus gave to his Apostles, in mind, because it is too easy for those in authority to become proud and overbearing, and believe, because they are in a role of responsibility, that they are in some way superior. Bishops and priests may have authority in the community, but, following Christ's example, it must be exercised in a spirit of humble service. In 595 Pope Gregory the Great applied to himself (and it was taken up and used by many popes after him) the title '*Servus servorum Dei*' (Servant of the servants of God).

Authoritative Guidance

The point being made here, in this chapter, is that, the average Catholic, in seeking to live a spiritual life, is not alone in that quest. It is easy, in exploring spirituality, to get lost in the bye-ways and exotic claims made by self-appointed 'guides' who set themselves up (see the few words on this in the Introduction). As we have seen the Catholic is a disciple of the Master, Christ Jesus, who is the head of his family, the Church. This worldwide community of the Baptised has leaders and spiritual guides appointed by Christ himself. These have the wise support and personal experience of the spiritual life of hundreds of saintly teachers, writers and spiritual guides, who have proved their authenticity and worth over the past 2,000 years; no Catholic is alone in their spiritual journey (see Appendix One for a list of some of these spiritual guides).

The bishop is the teaching authority in each Catholic diocese, but not every bishop is learned or saintly; some have even been public sinners, lacking the humility of Christ.

One outstanding, humble bishop, who proved himself to be a remarkable spiritual guide and writer, over many centuries, is Francis de Sales; his writings are still treasured.

Humble Spiritual guide

ST FRANCIS DE SALES (1567-1622)

Francis de Sales, was 19 years of age when Margaret Clitherow, the housewife and mother of York (see chapter 3) was crushed to death for her devotion to the Eucharist. It is unlikely that Francis ever heard of her, because he was born into a wealthy family of Savoy, and enjoyed an expensive education at the Sorbonne, Paris, and the university of Padua. However, like Margaret, he had a great devotion to the Blessed Sacrament. After ordination to the Catholic Priesthood, in 1593, he was sent on a mission to the largely Protestant region of Chablais, where faced with great personal danger and much suffering, he won over many of the Calvinists to Catholicism by his gentle charity and humble service of all. (Later in life his pet phrase was 'You achieve more with a spoonful of honey than a barrel full of vinegar'.) He was consecrated Bishop of Geneva in 1602. He fulfilled his role of teacher of the diocese, in a largely Protestant area, in a humble, gentle and conciliatory spirit, while never bending from a faithful delivery of the Catholic Faith.

His simple, yet searching book *An Introduction to the Devout Life* (1609) has been hailed as a spiritual classic and it has never, over 400 years, been out of print! His treatise *The Love of God* (1616) is more substantial, but just as valuable; both works had considerable influence on the direction and content of later spiritual writing. Francis de Salle was renowned for being firm and clear when he spoke, or wrote, with authority on doctrine and the spiritual life, but he was always humble, gentle and approachable. He was declared a Saint of the Church in 1665 and received the highest accolade of 'Doctor of the Church' in 1877.

SUMMARY

Without guidance people can be led astray or wander off; Christ provided that authoritative guidance by appointing his Apostles to be custodians of his teaching, under the inspiration of the Holy Spirit. Over the centuries the Bishops, the successors of the Apostles, have, under the leadership of the Bishop of Rome, continued that role of guardians and exponents of Christ's Good News. World-wide, in every Catholic church, the teaching and guiding role of the bishop is symbolised by the celebrant's chair. Apart from himself, only his authorised representative, the parish priest, may use that chair. Catholic spirituality is kept 'on track' by the teaching authority of the Church; this includes the respected writings and saintly example of hundreds of deceased faithful Church members, many of whom have been officially declared to be saints (see Appendix One).

NOTES – CHAPTER 6

1. *'From Age to Age'* by Edward Foley, p.70.
2. The Second Vatican Council's on the Bishops' Pastoral Office in the Church, p.397.

CHAPTER 7 *Focus:* THE FONT, THE CONFESSIONAL

REPENTANCE AND BAPTISM

The Font

Entering a church, or cathedral, built in the Middle Ages, you are likely to notice that the baptismal font is near to the main door. This positioning emphasised the belief that it is by Baptism that a person 'enters' the Church, in the sense of becoming a member. In the Catholic churches re-ordered, post-1965, to fulfil the directions of the liturgical reforms of the Second Vatican Council, you will find the font, either in a special **'baptistery'** area on its own, or up in the sanctuary, close to the altar and the ambo. The shape and design of the font has a long history, which reflects how the Church's teaching and practice of Baptism has developed over time.

Church's Birthday

On Pentecost Day, the day the Christian Church was born, at the end of Peter's first speech, or sermon, the people in the crowd were cut to the heart and said to Peter and the other apostles, "what are we to do, brothers?" "You must repent," Peter answered, "and everyone of you must be baptised in the name of Jesus Christ for the forgiveness of you sins" (Acts 3:38). The very first action of the nascent Church, following the proclamation of the Good News, was to baptise. A few verses further on we are told 'those who accepted his message were baptised, and about three thousand were added to their number that day' (v.41). The logistics of baptising such a large number of people – and in the city of Jerusalem – must have been very challenging and kept the eleven Apostles busy all that day!

A Change of Heart

Apart from the nativity stories in Matthew and Luke's Gospels, each of the three Synoptic Gospels opens with a call to repentance, and, as a sign of that repentance, acceptance of baptism, administered by John the Baptiser. In fact the first words that Mark places on the lips of Jesus is a call to repentance; 'The time has come, The kingdom of God is near. Repent and believe the Good News'. This opening is identical to Peter's proclamation and call to repentance and baptism, on Pentecost day. Christ asks for 'a change of heart' (*metanoia* in the original Greek), true sorrow for sin, with the acceptance of Baptism as a sign of that new life. No other way is proposed. Each individual person who wishes to live the Christian/Catholic spiritual life must start at the same point.

Meaning of Baptism

Pope Benedict XVI has written 'Water symbolism pervades the Gospel of John from beginning to end. We meet it for the first time in Jesus' conversation with Nicodemus in chapter 3. In order to be able to enter the Kingdom of God, (the Pope explains, earlier in his book, that this means accepting God as ruling in your life) man must be made anew, he must become another person – he must be born again of water and the Spirit' (cf. Jn 3:5). What does this mean? 'Baptism, the gateway into communion with Christ, is being interpreted for us here as rebirth. This rebirth – by analogy with natural birth from the begetting of the man and the conception of the woman – involves a double principle: God's Spirit and water. Putting it another way, rebirth involves the creative power of God's Spirit, but it also requires the sacrament of the maternal womb of the receiving and welcoming Church.'[1]

Sacramental Spirituality

Catholic Spirituality can be seen to be, pre-eminently, a sacramental spirituality; union with the Risen Christ grows and is deepened through the sacraments. (We have already seen in chapter three the centrality of the Eucharist.) Once Baptism has been received, in the name of the Father and of the Son and of the Holy Spirit, and one has been incorporated into the spiritual life of the Church, the Christian has a right to the other sacraments.

Expected Second Coming

The early Christians expected the imminent return of Christ in glory (later this was called the 'Second Coming') to judge the living and the dead and to terminate the present world order. So deep and solid was this belief that they sold their houses and property in readiness.

> 'The apostles continued to testify to the resurrection of the Lord Jesus with great power, and they were all accorded great respect. None of their members was ever in want, as all those who owned land or houses would sell them, and bring the money from the sale of them, to present it to the apostles; it was then distributed to any who might be in need' (Acts 4: 33-35).

The Sacrament of Penance

But Christ did not return and, despite their very best intentions, the baptised began to sin; some seriously. Without pursuing the problem, which racked the Church at that time over what to do, it opened the way to a new development. The problem was that Baptism was understood to be a once in a lifetime sacrament of repentance, that washed all sin away and marked the beginning of a new life of grace. So, the question was, should serious sinners, who had fallen from grace and failed to keep their baptismal promises, be expelled from the community? But where was the love and compassion of Christ in that solution, if the sinners repented and wanted to try again? As expulsion was not possible, the Church gradually developed the sacrament of Penance to deal with the problem. By the third century there had emerged a developed system of public Penance, which was regarded as a 'second Baptism'. After the sinner, voluntarily or under threat of excommunication, had asked the bishop for Penance, he was enrolled in the order of penitents, excluded from Communion (both Holy Communion and union with others in the community), and committed to a severe course of prayer, fasting, and almsgiving. At the end of the period, the length of which was determined by the gravity of the sin, the sinner was reconciled and rejoined the congregation of the faithful. Because of the severity of this regime the system eventually broke down and Penance was usually postponed until the eve of death. (It is said that the Emperor Constantine delayed his Baptism until his deathbed, for similar reasons.)

The Paschal Candle

Standing in the baptistery, or close to the font, the Easter or Paschal, Candle will be seen. Free-standing on the floor, the tall, often ornate, candlestick holds a tall candle which is decorated. Closer examination will reveal that the decorations, towards the top of the candle, consist of letters, numbers and brass 'nails' pushed into the candle.

The numbers indicate the year and the two Greek letters are alpha and omega, which stand for God the Beginning and the End (three times, in the Book of Revelation, God says 'I am the Alpha and the Omega' [cf. 1:8, 21:6 and 22:13]). The five brass 'nails', which are hollow and contain a few grains of incense, represent the five glorified wounds of Christ. The candle is blessed and first lit at the Easter Vigil; the light being taken from the new fire, which represents Christ rising from the dead.

Easter Vigil

At the Vigil service, which heralds in the great festival of Easter, the Easter Candle is borne into the darkened church. The deacon, or priest, carrying it stops three times and sings *Lumen Christi* ('Light of Christ'); then the people present light their candles from the Easter Candle. Light spreads dramatically through the darkened building. The readings and songs that follow all relate to 'fire' or 'water'; the latter because the baptismal water will be blessed that night and some converts may be baptised.

The Paschal candle, standing close to the altar, is lit during services in the Easter season. It is moved to be beside the font on the evening of Pentecost, or Whitsunday. There it is lit, representing Christ the Light of the world, for every Baptism. Each child baptised in that font in the coming year will receive a lighted candle, lit from the Paschal candle.

The Box

In most Catholic churches built before 1965 the visitor can still see at least one **confessional**. The original number of these around the building depended upon the size of the church, and therefore, in pre-Vatican II days, the size of the congregation and the number of expected penitents. Catholics of that era, and before, would familiarly refer to such a place for meeting the priest in secrecy, for the confessing of sins, as 'the box'.

Private Confession

The confessional spotlights individual confession, as distinct from general confession, which reflects the instruction found in the letter of James, 'confess your sins to one another' (5:16). General confession, made in public, for understandable reasons, did not catch on in the life of the Church. The idea of humbly confessing wrongdoing, but not the public profession of sin, does continue in a liturgical fashion at the beginning of each celebration of the Eucharist.

Private, individual, confession to a confessor (in modern times, to an ordained priest) did take root. This approach to the confession and repentance of sin emerged between the fifth and eighth centuries, in monastic communities, especially those of the Irish Celtic tradition. Here the emphasis was upon spiritual direction, a form of spiritual counsel that evolved and flourished with the rise of monasticism. The penitent would visit a spiritual confessor or director (increasingly over time a priest), make a confession of sin (this was called 'auricular confession') and then receive spiritual guidance and counsel. Developments continued over the centuries until the sixteenth century when the Council of Trent required individual auricular confession for all serious sin.

Saturday Confession

Prior to the beginning of the twentieth century Catholics very rarely received Holy Communion at Mass; principally because so many preachers had instilled into them a great awe of the Sacrament and a deep sense of unworthiness in approaching it. It was Pope Pius X (declared a saint in 1954) who worked hard to promote the regular reception of Holy Communion. In 1905 he emphasised the frequent approach to the Sacrament of Penance (Confession), so that Holy Communion would be received worthily. One of the Pope's favourite sayings was, 'Holy Communion is the shortest and safest way to Heaven'. The result of this campaign in the Church, spearheaded by the saintly Pope, was that people flocked to confession on a Saturday so that they were prepared to receive Holy Communion the next day. Priests would regularly spend three or four hours each Saturday sitting in the confessional.

Communion at every Mass

The reforms of the Church's worship, promulgated by the Second Vatican Council, encouraged reception of Holy Communion at every Mass;

> 'Hearty endorsement is given to that closer form of participation in the Mass whereby the faithful, after the priest's communion, receive the Lord's body under elements consecrated at that very sacrifice' (para 55).[2]

With this encouragement went the instruction – to prepare themselves for the Eucharist – to make more use of the penitential rite at the beginning of the Mass. The opening Rite was to allow the congregation time to consider their faults and failings and then share in a prayer of repentance, (the usual form used is the prayer which starts with the words, 'I confess...'). One unforeseen consequence of this greater familiarity of the people with the Eucharist, and the opening rite of repentance, has been the dramatic decline in the number of Catholics approaching the Sacrament of Reconciliation (as the Council's reforms renamed 'Penance' or 'Confession').

Reconciliation Rooms

The Liturgical reforms also instructed that, as an alternative to the confessional box, (one or two of which has been retained in most churches) that many people were uncomfortable with, every parish church should have a special small room set aside for administering the Sacrament of Reconciliation. In this room the penitent would be offered the choice of speaking to the priest face to face (as one does with one's medical doctor) or using a screen, so the identity of the penitent could remain a secret. There are still many Catholics who prefer the secure unanimity of the old confessional to the reconciliation room. Many people nowadays only celebrate the Sacrament during Advent, in preparation for Christmas, and during Lent, in preparation for Easter.

Water Stoup

The visitor to a Catholic church may notice, as she or he enters, that many of the people entering (some do it as they leave as well) dip their finger into water which is in a basin, called a **stoup**, just inside the church door. Then they trace the **Sign of the Cross** on themselves, as they say the words, 'In the name of the Father and of the Son and of the Holy Spirit', as a blessing. Although most Catholics execute this traditional practice, many do not realise that it is intended, in addition to being a blessing of themselves, to be a reminder of their own baptism, when water was poured on their head in the name of the Holy Trinity.

Before the reforms of the Second Vatican Council priests would spend many hours, especially on a Saturday, in the confessional; but none as many as the French priest, John Vianney. It is not possible to speak of saints and the confessional without making mention of the heroic sanctity of the Curé d'Ars, who pre-eminently was the saint of the Sacrament of Reconciliation.

Curé d'Ars

ST JOHN VIANNEY (1786-1859)

Jean-Marie-Baptiste Vianney was born into a large, poor, farming family, at Dardilly, near Lyons, France, in 1786. He wanted to be a priest from an early age, but he was growing up during the French Revolution and Catholic priests were hunted by the revolutionaries and executed if caught. It was a criminal offence to attend Mass so his family secretly went to the Eucharist in remote barns, with lookouts on alert for the gendarmes; Jean-Marie-Baptiste made his First Communion in such surroundings. Impressed by the saintly example of his parish priest, Charles Balley, he expressed the desire to be a priest and the Abbé Balley put him forward to train for the priesthood. However Jean had received scarcely any education and had serious difficulties with Latin; he consistently came last in all examinations. Believing deeply in the young man, Abbé Balley undertook to educate him privately; but even personal tuition did not get him through the exams necessary for ordination. Through an error he was conscripted into the Republican Army in 1809. Having signed up, Jean suffered a bout of sickness and was left behind, when his regiment moved off; trying to catch up, he became lost and he was declared to be a deserter. Jean hid with other deserters in a remote village called Les Noes, where, under an assumed name, he founded a simple village school.

A general amnesty for all deserters was passed in 1810 and this brought Jean-Marie-Baptiste out of hiding and into the seminary at Verrieres; but his problems with study persisted. Only testimonials of his personal sanctity secured his path to Ordination to the Priesthood, which took place in August 1815. He became the assistant priest to Abbé Balley, who had always been Jean's inspiration. On the Abbé's death he was appointed the parish priest, or Curé, of the remote village of Ars. (Ever afterwards he would be known, even to the present, as the Curé d'Ars).

Jean-Marie-Baptiste discovered, on arrival in his parish, that the Catholic Faith was not well practised in the village, for example, the people worked on Sundays; but he won many hearts and minds with his tender care of the sick and the poor. He founded a free school for destitute girls called 'The Providence'. He taught in the school himself and struggled for ten years to provide enough food and clothing for the destitute girls, who were boarding. Even though The Providence was forced to close in 1847, it became a model for similar institutions that were established all over France.

For a priest with such a poor educational background, the Curé d'Ars preached extraordinary sermons, full of the love of God. People began to travel long distances, even from Paris itself, to his remote village, to hear him preach and go to confession. He lived a very simple and an extremely austere life; struggling for thirty-five years with constant temptations. Any money which came his way, up to 1847, went directly to the feeding and clothing of the girls at The Providence. He was not unlike one of the Desert Fathers in his fasting, constant prayer and struggles with satanic temptations. He took on the harshest kinds of penance, on behalf of the sinners who came to him for confession. He said of this, 'I impose only a small penance on those who confess their sins properly; the rest I perform in their place'. His fame grew, and by 1855 the number of people making the journey to Ars, to hear him preach and go to confession was 20,000 a year. (To facilitate travel a French Railway company specially ran a branch line out to Ars). During the last ten years of his life he spent sixteen to eighteen hours a day in the confessional. Even the secular State acknowledged the immense impact of the humble and self-effacing Curé d'Ars, by awarding him the Imperial Order of the Legion d'Honneur. The first question the Abbé Vianney asked, when the local Mayor told him he was to receive the award, was: 'Is there a pension attached to that cross? Does it mean money for my poor?' 'No, it is just a distinction' came the reply. 'Very well, since the poor have nothing to gain from it, tell the Emperor, please, that I do not want it!'

Jean-Marie-Baptiste Vianney died age 73, on 4 August 1859. He was canonised in 1925. To celebrate the centenary of his death, in 1959, Pope John XXIII, in a special **encyclical** letter, named him the patron saint of parish priests. The encyclical tells of St John Vianney's constant concern for the poor, quoting him as saying, 'There are many people keeping their money hidden away while many others are dying of hunger'.

SUMMARY

The font stands prominently in the church as a reminder to parishioners of the important event of their Baptism; through which they became members of the community and sin was 'washed away'. Little progress can be made in the Spiritual life, without the regular acknowledgement that we sin. First, John the Baptist, then Christ himself, called on their followers to acknowledge that they were sinners, have 'a change of heart' and repent. This call went out from Peter on the first day of the Church; it remains the constant call of Christ to his followers. The sacrament of Reconciliation (Penance or Confession) developed to bring Christ's forgiveness to repentant sinners; it has changed, over the years, in format, but remains powerfully the same essential sacrament.

NOTES – CHAPTER 7

1. *Jesus of Nazareth* by Pope Benedict XVI, p.239.
2. The Second Vatican Council's Constitution on the Sacred Liturgy, p.156.

CHAPTER 8   *Focus:* THE TABERNACLE

THE HIDDEN PRESENCE

The Tabernacle

If our imaginary visitor to a Catholic church had made their visit before 1965, as we have already indicated, things would have looked rather differently inside the building. The altar would have been attached to the back wall of the sanctuary, with, rising up above it, a highly decorated **reredos**. Standing on the altar, in the centre of the reredos, would have been seen the tabernacle; above which there would be a shelf, usually occupied by a free-standing crucifix. The latter would be removed, when there was to be a service of **Benediction** of the Blessed Sacrament, for on that shelf the **monstrance** would be placed, for all to see. All of these – 'reredos', 'tabernacle', 'Benediction', 'monstrance' – were essential parts of a popular love and adoration of the Blessed Sacrament, that had gradually developed from the end of the twelfth century.

The Sacring

Eamon Duffy, in *The Stripping of the Altars,* an important examination of traditional Religion in England between 1440 and 1580, tells of this adoration of the Blessed Sacrament. Popular preachers, over time, had so emphasised the sacredness of the consecrated host and the unworthiness of churchgoers, that they rarely received Holy Communion. Instead there was the 'sacring', which was the public worship of the moment of consecration and the elevation of the Host, which took place immediately after the celebrating priest had, in the context of the Mass, uttered the 'sacred' words of Christ. Duffy explains the long-established practice:

> 'Everyone received Holy Communion at Easter, and one's final communion, the viaticum or "journey money" given on the deathbed, was crucially important to medieval people. ...But for most people, most of the time the Host was something to be seen, not to be consumed. Since the end of the twelfth century it had been customary for the consecrating priest to elevate the Host high above his head immediately after the sacring (the repetition of the words of institution), *"Hoc est enim Corpus Meum"* (This is my Body), which brought about the miracle of **transubstantiation** for adoration by the people. Just before the sacring in every Mass a bell was rung to warn worshippers, absorbed in their prayers, to look up, because the moment of consecration was near...'[1]

Dr Duffy tells how the church bells were rung as the priest elevated the Host, so that people in the streets around the church could run to the church and see the elevation, which the priest would hold up for as long as possible, so that all might get there to see. He records that 'to see the Host, however fleetingly, was a privilege bringing blessing'. And people of that time were hungry for blessings because of the constant fears they entertained of death and final judgement.

Peter Ackroyd in his *The Life of Thomas More* describes the extremes that people went to, in order to witness the elevation of the host:

> 'At that instant candles and torches, made up of bundles of wood, were lit to illuminate the scene; the sacring bell was rung, and the church bells pealed

so that those in the neighbouring streets or fields might be aware of the solemn moment. ...The worshippers knelt down and held out their arms in adoration, since this was the sight for which they had come. There are reports of the people running from altar to altar to catch a glimpse of the consecrated host at different Masses, and one priest complained that at the sound of the sacring bell the people rushed away from his sermon to witness the elevation.'[2]

Distorted Pious Practice

This indicates how popular preaching, followed by popular devotional spirituality, had put so much emphasis upon the sacredness of the consecrated bread and wine – it was believed to be truly the Body and Blood of Christ, really present – that ordinary folk were not deemed worthy to receive Holy Communion, but only fit to see and adore. So the practice had altered considerably from the early years of Christianity, when a communal meal presided over by an apostle, elder or presbyter, concluded with the Eucharist, in imitation of what Christ had done at the Last Supper. It is clear from Scripture that the consecrated elements of bread *and* wine were never intended to be removed from the setting of a sacred memorial meal, to stand alone for an out of context, exaggerated adoration.

Restoring the Eucharist

It was not until the Liturgical reforms of the Second Vatican Council that the balance was restored. It is essential here to make clear that the adoration of the Blessed Sacrament is a very good practice – many saints, like Charles de Foucauld and St Joseph Labre, (see below) developed their close relationship with Christ and achieved outstanding sanctity through such a devotion – but the primary focus of the Eucharist, as intended by Christ, is as sacred food and drink in the context of a memorial meal; this is believed, by Catholics, to be both a sacrifice and a sacrament. Naturally it is an act of public worship, but one which can prompt and develop private prayer and worship.

Reservation valued

The reserving of the consecrated bread (the sacred wine is never kept and stored) in the special, secure and ornate cupboard, called a tabernacle, is encouraged by the Church. As the following extract makes clear, the reservation is for two purposes: first and foremost, for taking Holy Communion, outside of Mass times, to the sick. Secondly, for personal prayer and silent adoration, before the tabernacle.

The Bishops of England and Wales write:

> At Mass and afterwards, Catholics express their faith in the real presence of Christ by genuflecting or bowing deeply as a sign of adoration. The radical conversion of the inner reality of the bread and wine means that the consecrated elements remain the 'Blessed Sacrament' of Christ's presence when the celebration of the Eucharist is over. Any remaining consecrated hosts are treated with the utmost reverence. For Catholics, reservation of the Blessed Sacrament is 'a sign of Christ's abiding presence in the Church and a much-loved focus of devotion'. Always centred on the actual celebration of the Eucharist, the sacrament is reserved for taking communion to the sick and for silent adoration' (para 55).[3]

The Catholic Catechism adds:

> 'In his Eucharistic presence Christ remains mysteriously in our midst as the one who loved us

and gave himself up for us, and he remains under signs that express and communicate this love' (para 1380).[4]

The English and Welsh Bishops make plain that:

We wish strongly to encourage prayer before the Blessed Sacrament: this includes extended periods of Exposition, Benediction and personal visits to church for prayerful adoration' (para 55).[5]

Religious dedicated to adoration

Some Religious communities of nuns, like the Handmaids of the Blessed Sacrament, who have a convent in Kensington, London; and the Adorers of the Sacred Heart, who are in Marylebone, London (their convent, in Hyde Park Place, is on the site of the old Tyburn gallows, where many Catholics were hung-dawn and quartered for their faith in the Eucharist, under Elizabeth I) base their prayer life on the Adoration of the Blessed Sacrament. There are also confraternities and pious associations, for example the Jesus Caritas Fraternity of Priests, (one of the foundations that come from the heritage of Charles de Foucauld and his Little Brothers of Jesus) have adoration before the Blessed Sacrament as an essential part of their devotional life.

Tabernacle: focus for adoration

It can be seen how tabernacles came to develop in the late seventeenth and early eighteenth centuries. They fulfilled a double role; first as a secure 'cupboard' for the consecrated hosts left over after a recent Mass, making it possible to take Holy Communion, as the need arose, to the sick. Secondly, for the reserved sacrament, particularly a large

Host kept in readiness for exposition and adoration at the service called 'Benediction'. The tabernacle became the focus for private prayer and adoration. The Catholic Catechism clearly spells out the Church's thinking:

> The tabernacle was first intended for the reservation of the Eucharist in a worthy place so that it could be brought to the sick and those absent, outside of Mass. As faith in the real presence of Christ in his Eucharist deepened, the Church became conscious of the meaning of silent adoration of the Lord present under the Eucharistic species. It is for this reason that the tabernacle should be located in an especially worthy place in the church, and should be constructed in such a way that it emphasises and manifests the truth of the real presence of Christ in the Blessed Sacrament' (para 1379).[6]

Forty Hours Devotion

About 1527, in Milan, Italy, a form of devotion called Quante 'Ore (or **Forty Hours**) was introduced. The idea spread rapidly and became very popular throughout Europe. It consisted in having exposition of the Blessed Sacrament for a continuous period of forty hours (a significant religious number, eg the Hebrews, wandered for forty years in the desert and Jesus spent forty days in the wilderness etc.) having the attendance, for unbroken adoration, of a stream of worshippers, all day and all night.

When evening Masses were permitted in the 1960s, and the Second Vatican Council's Decree on the Liturgy deepened everyone's understanding of the central role and place of the Eucharist in the spiritual life, the provision of exposition of the Blessed Sacrament and Quante 'Ore in parishes declined. However, in the 1990s there has been – encouraged by the publication of *One Bread One Body* – a renewed appreciation and evaluation, in many places, of the spiritual value of silent prayer before the Blessed Sacrament, exposed for adoration. Many parishes now provide, in the course of the week, a period of exposition of the Blessed Sacrament and adoration before it, for personal prayer and reflection.

Communion to the Sick

During the time of the Roman persecutions of the Church, in the first three centuries, it was common practice for one or two members of the community to take the consecrated bread from the local Eucharistic gathering, to those in prison, or to the sick. There are many traditional stories of the heroism of such Christians, some of whom ended up in prison themselves, and losing their lives. Like much else in the life of the Church, over the centuries, this charitable act became reserved to the clergy. So, before the liturgical reforms of the Second Vatican Council it was only the priest who was permitted to take out the Eucharist to sick and housebound parishioners. This meant that few could benefit and there could be no obvious connection made and demonstrated with the community's act of worship; which the sick person was absent from. The Council restored the practice of duly commissioned lay people taking out the Eucharist, directly from the parish Mass. It is a common sight, nowadays, to see lay people, commissioned as extraordinary ministers of the Eucharist, coming forward, at Holy Communion time, to collect the consecrated host (the wine is never taken) and being dispatched, by the celebrant, to the sick and housebound, with a blessing. For many of those who benefit, this is an essential lifeline to their community and to their personal spiritual lives.

Very many saints have appreciated and grown in their spiritual lives through personal adoration before the Blessed Sacrament. However few have had the time to spend, over many years, whole days in adoration. One unusual exception was the saintly beggar, Benedict Labre, whose time was his own.

'The Beggar of Rome'

ST BENEDICT LABRE (1748-1783)

Sleeping by night in the ruins of the Colosseum in Rome, 'the Beggar of Rome' as Benedict Labre was popularly known by Romans, spent most of his day in church. Born into a prosperous family of fifteen children, near Boulogne, France, in 1748, Benedict was the eldest son. He did not want to follow in the family shop-keeping business, instead, after a good education, he felt called to the Religious life. Between 1766 and 1770 he made several attempts to join a number of Religious Orders, like the Carthusians and the Cistercians. He was continually rejected as unsuitable. Then he discovered his true vocation as a mendicant pilgrim. In 1770 he began a pilgrimage on foot to Rome, living on what he could beg. For the next four years, on his way to Rome, he visited all the principal shrines, Compostella in Spain; Loreto, Bari and Assisi in Italy; Einsiedeln in Switzerland; Aix-en-Provence and Paray-le-Monial in France. He always travelled on foot, slept in the open or in some street corner. He was not concerned about the rags he wore and shared any money or food he was given with other beggars he met. He talked little, prayed unceasingly and accepted the regular abuse he encountered without murmur. Eventually, in 1774, arriving in Rome, he slept in the ruins of the Colosseum at night and spent his days praying in the churches; seeking out those that were celebrating the Forty Hours devotion, which he loved and did what he could to promote. Benedict would kneel for hours silently before the Blessed Sacrament; his example had a profound effect upon hundreds of people. He was well known in Rome for his sanctity; viewed by people as a 'new St Francis of Assisi'. After some years failing health forced him to take up residence in a home for the destitute. At length, before the Blessed Sacrament, that he loved so much to adore, he collapsed in church, and died in the back room of a nearby butcher's shop, to which he had been carried. He was, by popular acclaim, declared a saint, long before he was officially canonised in 1881.

SUMMARY

The tabernacle exists for the storage of the consecrated hosts, so that Holy Communion may be taken to the sick, and as the focal point of private adoration to the reserved Sacrament. Adoration of the Eucharist – particularly during the elevation at Mass – developed to an extreme form in the Middle Ages, due to preachers warning the people of their sinful unworthiness to receive Holy Communion; so reception was a rare event. The Second Vatican Council restored Christ's original intention ('Take and eat' and 'Take and drink') to the Church; and encouraged reception of Holy Communion at every Mass attended. Exposition and adoration of the Blessed Sacrament have, in recent years, been encouraged once again, but no longer as a substitute for receiving Holy Communion.

NOTES – CHAPTER 8

1. *The Stripping of the Altars* by Eamon Duffy, p.95.
2. *The Life of Thomas More* by Peter Ackroyd, p.110.
3. *One Bread, One Body* by the Bishops of England and Wales, pp.36-7.
4. *Catechism of the Catholic Church*, p.311.
5. *One Bread, One Body* by the Bishops of England and Wales, p.37.
6. *Catechism of the Catholic Church*, p.311.

CHAPTER 9   *Focus:* THE CRUCIFIX

CROSS OR CRUCIFIX?

Crucifix, sign of love

Most Catholic churches have, prominently displayed behind or above the altar, a large **crucifix**. This is intended to be a reminder, to all who see it, of the immeasurable love of Christ, that prompted him to make the sacrifice of his life for humankind. While the practice of hanging a crucifix in the church has a long history, it cannot be traced back to the early centuries of Christianity. The Christians of the first five centuries knew nothing of using the crucifix in any way at all; it had too many horrific, nightmare associations for them. Right up until the Emperor Constantine banned the capital punishment of crucifixion in 337 AD, the idea never occurred to Christians to be anything but totally horrified by the cross with a figure on it.

Cross triumphant

However in the third century the cross (as distinct from the crucifix) was adapted to be used as a symbol; but not on its own. Carvings, engravings and catacomb drawings have survived showing a plain cross with a victor's laurel wreath, or crown, carved or drawn above it. The inspiration for this was from a well-known contemporary practice. In the Roman Empire, during the lives of the Apostles, and throughout the first few centuries of the Christian era, victorious Roman emperors would conduct showy, spectacular, 'triumphs' through the streets of Rome. The emperor, in his white chariot, would have a slave, standing behind him, holding the laurel wreath of the victor, over his head, as the military procession of resplendent legions, preceding columns of humiliated, captive enemies, threaded its way through the packed streets to the Forum. The victor's crown was the symbol of the emperor's triumph over enemies, suffering and death. So Christians adopted the idea, recognising that by his resurrection Christ hadbeen the victor over suffering and death; so a plain empty cross was headed by a victor's wreath.

Passion imagery

While the story of Christ's Passion and death was regularly re-visited at each weekly Eucharist, there was no popular devotional use of the Passion story in the first 1,000 years. Imagery based on the Passion of Christ became increasingly popular and common from the thirteenth century. The ground for this was prepared by the immensely influential writings of the Cistercian monk and **Doctor** of the Church, St Bernard of Clairvaux (1090-1153). Statues and pictures of the saint regularly showed him with the symbols of the sufferings of Christ, namely the crown of thorns, the nails etc. The other powerful influence was the religious renewal brought about by the followers of St Francis of Assisi. Both he and Saint Bernard placed a special emphasis on the humanity of Christ and encouraged an 'affective' spirituality, which concentrated on the Passion. 'Human compassion, the natural sense of sympathy and pity for the suffering of others, could be harnessed to inspire and deepen faith in Christ and to strengthen devotion to him. The image of Christ on the cross was no longer solely the sign of God's love and his sacrifice for humanity; it became the focus of humanity's own compassion for the suffering Saviour.'[1]

Impact of the Mystics

The English **Mystics** of the fourteenth century, for example Richard Rolle (d.1349) in his *The Fire of Love* and Walter Hilton (d.1396) in his *The Scale of Perfection*, bring a fresh and new emphasis on union, in love, with the person of Jesus and a close empathy with him.

> 'Jesus is united to a man's soul by goodwill and by a deep desire to possess him alone, and see him spiritually in his glory. The stronger this desire, the closer the union between Jesus and the soul: the weaker this desire, the looser the union. Any spirit or experience that weakens this desire and distracts the soul from constant thought of Jesus Christ and its proper aspirations for him will damage and disrupt this union between Jesus and the soul.'[2]

Influence of St Francis of Assisi

The preaching of the Franciscan Friars, throughout Christendom, was more influential than the writings of the Catholic mystics. Naturally, St Francis, himself, was their inspiration and their founder and he had a great devotion to Christ in his Passion. St Francis prayed to God the Father, that he might feel the pain and grief that Christ felt in his Passion and he was rewarded with the **stigmata**, the wounds that Christ bore on his body at the Crucifixion. 'This episode is the most frequently represented in the cycles of the life of St Francis, since it is the one that most completely demonstrated his conformity to Christ.'[3]

Saint Francis was not the only saint to seek such an intimate closeness to Christ, St Catherine of Siena, in the following century, also expressed the desire to be united to Christ in his Passion. She appealed for this in prayer. According to her biographer, Raymond of Capua, her request was granted.

'The painting by the seventeenth-century artist, Rutilio Manetti shows St Catherine receiving the stigmata; remarkably though, she receives them not from a vision of Christ but from a painted medieval crucifix. During her meditation on the image she had been overtaken by ecstasy, causing her to faint. Manetti's painting is an eloquent testimony to the power of the religious image in the context of Passion meditation'.[4]

The Five Wounds of Christ

And so the crucifix became the icon of the Western Church and placed in a central position in all Catholic places of worship. (In modern times, for example, a crucifix, or sometimes a cross in a modern style, will be seen hanging in every classroom in a Catholic school.) In England, during the late Middle Ages, a devotion to the Five Wounds of Christ – the wounds in his hands, feet and side – developed and became very popular. Eamon Duffy tells us:

> 'Devotion to the Wounds of Jesus was one of the most popular cults of late medieval Europe, and in England it was growing in popularity up to the eve of the Reformation.'[5]

He continues with pages of detail on the prayer books, which contained a wide selection of prayers to the Wounds.

> 'The side wound of Christ had a particular fascination and devotional power, for it gave access to the heart, and thereby became a symbol of refuge in his love. **Julian of Norwich** was shown, in her tenth revelation, the Wound in Christ's side, and says there resides "a feye and delectable place, and large jnow for alle mankynde that shalle be savyd and rest in pees and in love".'[6]

The Sign of the Cross

From the earliest times individual Christians had made the sign of the cross on themselves. Tertullian, the African Father of the Church, writing in 218 AD, says,

> 'At every forward step and movement, at every going in and out, when we put on our clothes and shoes ... in all the ordinary actions of everyday life, we trace the sign of the cross.'[7]

This practice began with a small cross, signed with the thumb of the right hand on the forehead, but developed later into touching the forehead, the lower chest and each shoulder, while saying the words 'In the name of the Father and of the Son and of the Holy Spirit'. The original intention of this devotional practice was for the Christian to be reminded of their baptism, in the name of the Blessed Trinity. With the gradual development of the devotion to the Wounds of Christ, the intention changed and the wounds of Christ were brought to mind as the person signed him/herself.

Cross or Crucifix?

Those who led the Protestant Reformation of the sixteenth century, intent upon returning to the simplicity of the early days of Christianity, as recorded in the Scriptures, rejected the crucifix; and some rejected the cross. Those who did use a plain, empty cross in their churches taught that it's message was that Christ had come down from the cross; he was risen. At the Second Vatican Council the emphasis in many of the documents was upon the Resurrection and the Easter Mysteries of Christ's conquest of death and his glorious resurrection. As a consequence, in many of the new churches built post-Vatican II, and some of those that were re-ordered, the traditional crucifix was replaced with the figure of Christ the King or Christ as Priest, reigning in majesty, from the cross; or an image on the cross that suggested the Risen Christ.

Congregation dedicated to the Passion

Paul Francis Danei (1694-1775) of Ovada, Italy, led a life of prayer and great austerity. In 1720 he had a number of mystical experiences, during which he felt the call to found a **congregation** of men totally dedicated to the Passion of Our Lord.

After many trials and difficulties the Rule for the Congregation of Discalced Clerks of the Most Holy Cross and Passion of our Lord Jesus Christ (always popularly known as 'Passionists') was approved by Pope Benedict XIII in 1741. It soon spread throughout Europe and arrived in England in 1841. The Passionists, in addition to the usual three vows of poverty, chastity and obedience, take the additional vow to further the memory of Christ's Passion; principally through the parish missions and the **retreats** that they conduct.

The most famous Passionist priest in England in the nineteenth century, Fr Dominic Barberi, lived his calling – to further the memory of Christ's Passion – so perfectly that he inspired one of the greatest intellectuals of the period, John Henry Newman, to become a Catholic. Newman would have no one else but Fr Barberi receive him into the Catholic Church.

The Apostle of England

BLESSED DOMINIC BARBERI (1792-1849)

It is humiliating to be laughed at for your odd looks, for being foreign, speaking English with an accent and for being an Italian Catholic in an unwelcoming Protestant country. Fr Dominic Barberi, during his seven years in England, endured it all with a smile. It was all welcomed by him as a sharing in the sufferings of Christ; for meditation on his Passion and death formed an integral part of Fr Barberi's spiritual life.

Born in 1792 of a poor Italian farming family, Dominic was an orphan by the age of eight. An uncle and aunt in the town of Merlano raised him and left him with the daily task of tending their sheep. Since his relatives thought that no education was necessary for a shepherd, Dominic taught himself to read and write. When Napoleon closed all religious houses in France and Italy, some Passionist priests, living in hiding in Merlano, befriended Dominic. They helped with his education and he became attracted to their way of life. Escaping the draft into the Army, and a marriage arranged for him by his uncle and aunt, Dominic had a religious experience that directed him to join the Passionist Congregation and gave him the idea that one day he would go to far-away England.

Dominic joined the novitiate, took his first vows and studied hard, revealing a brilliant mind. He was ordained a priest in Rome on 1 March 1821. For the next nineteen years he taught philosophy and theology to young students for the Priesthood; but his mind constantly returned to the thought of going to England; the desire would not go away.

The Passionist Congregation made the decision to found a religious house in England and Dominic, despite poor health, was asked to go. First he was instructed to found a house in Belgium and, finally, after twenty-eight years of effort, he arrived in England. Eventually, in 1841, Dominic established the first Passionist house in England at Aston Hall, Staffordshire. The Passionists were the first religious, after the Reformation, to lead a strict community life and wear their habit in public. (This led to considerable abuse.)

Fr Dominic won the hearts of many by the indomitable courage and simple faith that he displayed in his activities among the poor Catholics in the factory towns of the Potteries. In his seven years of hard, tireless, missionary work in England (during which time he was called 'the Apostle of England') Dominic established another three houses for his Congregation. His powerful preaching, letter-writing and in depth discussions with Protestant academics, which were founded on his daily meditations on the sufferings of Christ in his Passion, won many converts. These included John Henry Newman, later Cardinal, and the Honourable George Spencer (great, great uncle of Diana, Princess of Wales), who became a Passionist and was later known as Fr Ignatius. (His cause for sainthood is currently going forward). Fr Dominic died suddenly and unexpectedly at a small railway station near Reading. He was buried under the altar of St Anne's Retreat, Sutton, St Helen's, England. He was beatified on 27 October 1963.

SUMMARY

The crucifix, the reminder of Christ's immeasurable love, was not an essential Christian symbol for the first 1,000 years of Christianity. It was the influence of the Catholic mystics and saints, particularly St Francis of Assisi that brought it to prominence; in the Middle Ages this was accompanied by devotion to the Five Wounds of Christ as well. The sign of the cross traced upon an individual Christian was first used in the third century. Modern churches, especially since the Second Vatican Council, often have a cross that signifies not the death but the resurrection of Christ.

NOTES – CHAPTER 9

1. *The Image of Christ* Exhibition catalogue, National Gallery, p.107.
2. *The Fire and the Cloud* edited by David Fleming, p.152.
3. *The Image of Christ* Exhibition catalogue, National Gallery, p.107.
4. *The Image of Christ* Exhibition catalogue, National Gallery, p.107.
5. *The Stripping of the Altars* by Eamon Duffy, p.238.
6. *The Stripping of the Altars* by Eamon Duffy, p.244.
7. *De Corona Militis* by Tertullian, quoted in *A Dictionary of Liturgy and Worship*, p.185.

CHAPTER 10   *Focus:* THE LADY CHAPEL

MARY, THE MOTHER OF GOD

Dedicated to the Virgin Mary

Many of the former Catholic churches in England and Wales, that were built before the Reformation, that is before the 1530s, were dedicated to St Mary the Virgin. (Of the 6,000 plus churches, 2,010 carry the name, in one form or other, of the Blessed Virgin.) This is not surprising since devotions to Mary proliferated in late Medieval England, as elsewhere in Christian Europe, and 'indeed Englishmen were encouraged to think of their country as being in a special way "Mary's Dowry", a notion propagated, for example, by the custodians of the shrine at **Walsingham**. Her cult came second only to that of Christ himself, and towered above that of all other saints'.[1]

'On 19 January 1511 the young King Henry VIII arrived at the shrine of the Virgin Mary at Walsingham to give thanks for the birth, three weeks earlier, of a son, Henry Prince of Wales. He was the latest and, as it turned out, the last of a long line of English kings to visit the shrine.' Henry VIII would remain a pious devotee of Our Lady of Walsingham for two thirds of his reign. When the King's men came to destroy the shrine twenty-six years later, they found there a candle still burning, which was maintained at the cost of the King, in perpetual intercession for the birth of a son (Henry, the Prince of Wales, having died on 22 February 1511). The King's pilgrimage and intercession of Our Lady of Walsingham was absolutely characteristic of people of the late Middle Ages, 'almost anyone who prayed at all, prayed to Mary'.[2]

European Devotion to Mary

Devotion to Mary had begun to blossom throughout Europe in the twelfth century, and the growth of the fame of the shrine at Walsingham, the boom in painting, book production, music and architecture, all bear witness to Mary's growing centrality in the Christian imagination. From the late twelfth century onwards, there were elaborate Lady Chapels added to the country's cathedrals and great churches. In these, and in many parish churches, by the fifteenth century, the daily singing of the evening antiphon to the Virgin Mary, the *Salve,* had become very popular. It was also at this time that the most popular of all devotions to Our Lady emerged – the **rosary**.

The *Angelus*

About this time the **Angelus** was introduced. Daniel O'Leary gives witness to its continuing popularity in Ireland.

> 'When I go back to Ireland I'm struck by the Angelus broadcast on television. It is a valiant effort to recover a kind of timing and fine-tuning of the way we are present to whatever we are doing at that moment. At twelve and at six, the bells are tolled. During the pealing, workers from a variety of professions are depicted as lifting their heads and pausing for the length of a few breaths. You sense they have shifted their awareness to another place. They have moved, for a moment, inside themselves, drawn to a horizon deep within their own soul. It does not seem to be so much a distraction as a way of living more fully in the present moment and devoted to the immediate work of their hands and eyes.'[3]

Mary of Nazareth

The facts about the historical Mary of Nazareth are few in number. The name by which she was known by her family and friends was Miryam or Miriam, which when the Gospels were written in Greek, and later translated into Latin, became 'Maria'; from which, of course, we get 'Mary'. She was named after Miriam, the sister of Moses and it was, at that time, a very common name for girls. Each had to have some addition to their name to distinguish them. So, in the Gospels we have Mary of Magdala (also known as Magdalene), Mary, the mother of James, Mary, the wife of Clopas and Mary of Bethany, sister of Lazarus.

Miriam came from Nazareth, a village in the hills of Galilee, with a population of between 1,600 and 2,000. They did not enjoy a good reputation! ('Nazareth', commented Nathaniel, 'can anything good come from that place?' [Jn 1:45]) The villagers were mainly employed in agriculture, although some, like Yosef (Joseph), to whom Miriam became engaged, had a trade. This, in Matthew's Gospel (13:55), is described by the Greek word *tekton*, which is usually translated as 'woodworker'. Their marriage would have been arranged; as all marriages were at the time. (No doubt love grew with the passing of time.) It was the practice for the engagement, or betrothal, to take place when the girl was between twelve and thirteen years of age. Since Miriam was found to be pregnant (see Luke 1:26-38) during the year which usually preceded the actual wedding ceremony, she was little more than thirteen years of age when she gave birth to Yeshua (Jesus) at Bethlehem. Miriam could hardly have had a more humble beginning – from a poor family (unless one believes later legends about her) from a derided rural village, and giving birth at a very young age, far from home, in a stable. In spite of this, by God's plan, Mary was destined to become the most famous woman of human history; but we have no idea what she looked like, how tall or short she was, when her birthday was, what she wore, who her friends were, and so on.

The references to Mary in the New Testament are few, and these have been expertly drawn together in the Agreed Statement between the Catholic and Anglican members of **ARCIC**.

> 'The scriptural witness summons all believers in every generation to call Mary 'blessed'; this Jewish woman of humble status, this daughter of Israel living in hope of justice for the poor, whom God has graced and chosen to become the virgin mother of his Son through the overshadowing of the Holy Spirit. We are to bless her as the 'handmaid of the Lord' who gave her unqualified assent to the fulfilment of God's saving plan, as the mother who pondered all things in her heart, as the refugee seeking asylum in a foreign land, as the mother pierced by the innocent suffering of her own child, and as the woman to whom Jesus entrusted his friends. We are at one with her and the apostles, as they pray for the outpouring of the Spirit upon the nascent Church, the eschatological family of Christ. And we may even glimpse in her the final destiny of God's people to share in her son's victory over the powers of evil and death' (para 30).[4]

Mary in the Early Church

In the early Church, reflection on Mary was bound up closely with reflection upon her Son. Controversy raged in the first five centuries over the identity of Christ; how could he be totally human, if he were divine, and how could he be divine, if he were completely a man, with a man's limited knowledge? In other words, who precisely was Christ? Was he a divine person, pretending to be a human being, or a human adopted by God? And in what sense could one say that Jesus was 'divine', when Judaism taught that there was only one God? It took 400 years to clarify in precise theological terms who the condemned man who died on Calvary was. The Council of Bishops gathered at Chalcedon, in Asia Minor (modern Turkey), in the year 451 AD, definitively taught that Jesus, the Christ, was one Person, (the Second Person of the Blessed Trinity) having two natures. The nature of God, being of the same substance as the Father, and human nature, being of the same substance as us. Having made this clear, the Council then went on to declare that the Virgin Mary was to be accorded the title *Theotokos* (the Council proceedings were conducted in Greek), which literally means 'the one who gave birth to God', or 'Mother of God'.

Devotion to Mary begins

In point of fact, this title 'Mother of God' for the Virgin Mary had already been used some twenty years earlier at the Council of Ephesus; but it was at Chalcedon that the relationship with her divine Son, the Second Person of the Holy Trinity, was made crystal clear.

The wonder of Christians, first of the East and then, a little later, of the Western Church, which accompanied the formal doctrinal pronouncement of the Council prompted the beginning of devotion to Mary. For, from the simple, poor, peasant life of an obscure Galilean village, God had elevated an apparently insignificant young thirteen-year-old girl to the most dignified and wondrous role of Mother of the Incarnate Word of God. Within a short time, in the East, icons were being painted of the Mother of God with her child on her arm.

> 'The practice of believers asking Mary to intercede for them with her son grew rapidly following her being declared *Theotokos* at the Council of Ephesus.

The most common form today of such intercession is the **Hail Mary**' (para 67).[5]

The Hail Mary

The Marian prayer familiar to all Catholics, and an essential part of the **Rosary**, is made up of two parts. The first half consists of two quotations from Scripture and the second part merely asks Mary, the *Theotokos,* to pray for us. The prayer was thrown out by the Protestant Reformers, in the sixteenth century, and it is still shunned by Evangelical Christians. It is a little bewildering to understand why this should be, since most of the prayer is straight from the Bible. First, we have the words of the angel Gabriel, 'Hail, Mary, full of grace, the Lord is with thee' (Lk 1:28). These words are immediately followed by those of Elizabeth in Luke 1:42 'Blessed art thou among women, and blessed is the fruit of thou womb, Jesus'. (The only addition made to the words of Scripture is the name 'Jesus'.) The second part consists of these words: 'Holy Mary, Mother of God, pray for us sinners now and at the hour of our death'. The title *Theotokos,* (Mother of God) as we have already noted, comes from the Council of Chalcedon in 451. This Council, and its teaching, was fully accepted by the sixteenth century Reformers; so there should be no problem about addressing Mary, as 'Mother of God', for indeed she was the mother of Jesus, who was human and divine. There is a long tradition, among all Christians, of asking others to pray for them; so there should be no problem with asking Mary, the first disciple of Christ, to pray for us; both now and at the hour of our death (see **Holy Death Spirituality**).

Icons and statues of the Mother of God

Every Orthodox church, whether Coptic, Greek or Russian, has at least one icon of Mary, the Mother of God, prominently displayed. There are hundreds of different styles of these icons of Mary, but the great majority of them show the Virgin Mother with her Son on her arm. Every Catholic church, of whatever age or style of architecture, has a Lady chapel or, at the very least, one statue or picture of the Blessed Virgin Mary, or Our Lady, as she is more familiarly known. The style of the statue can vary considerably, according to local history or devotion. The most familiar statue seen in Catholic churches is of Our Lady of Lourdes (see story below), where the Blessed Virgin stands alone and is portrayed wearing a long white gown, with a blue waist sash. Seen a little less often, in churches, is a statue of Our Lady of Fatima, (an important shrine in Portugal) which shows Mary wearing a full length white gown, trimmed with gold; and she wears a small gold crown on her head.

English shrine of Walsingham

Occasionally the statue in the church will be of Our Lady of Walsingham; a Shrine in the village of Little Walsingham in north Norfolk. This shows Mary sitting on a throne with the Divine Child on her lap. She is dressed as a woman of the Middle Ages with a simple gold crown on her head and a tall white lily (symbolising purity) in her right hand, which also points to her Son, who sits on her lap. There are, occasionally, statues, or pictures, of Our Lady that are not a reminder of any one of her many apparitions (see Appendix Three), but are carved in wood or stone and inspired by an event in her life or some insight of the artist. One fine example of such is in the chapel of the Franciscan Sisters of the Divine Motherhood, at Godalming, Surrey. There, in the entrance hall, is a touching, beautiful stone statue, and behind the altar, a colourful mosaic, of the Mother of God breast-feeding the Child Jesus.

Misunderstandings about Mary

There has been, over the centuries, (particularly since the preaching of the Reformers of the sixteenth century) some misunderstanding about Catholic devotion to Mary, the Mother of God. Critics have accused Catholics of praying to Mary as though she was equal with Christ, as God. Knowledgeable Catholics are quick to correct this distortion of the true teaching regarding *Theotokos*.

First it has to be said that seeking the intercession of Mary, and according her a special place of honour, as the mother of the Son of God, began and became firmly established in the Church of the East, long before it spread to Europe and particularly England and Wales. It is possible for good practices to be abused by a largely uneducated populace that does not understand theology. Undoubtedly, there were some abuses in the England of the late Middle Ages by an over-exaggerated emphasis upon Mary's place and role. However, Dr Duffy, in *Stripping the Altars,* the Documents of the Second Vatican Council and the Agreed Statement on Mary between the Catholic Church and the Anglican Communion, give a much more balanced picture:

> 'Mother of Mercy was one of Mary's most resonant medieval titles, unforgettably carved, painted, or engraved, extending her sheltering cloak over the suppliant faithful and enshrined in the most haunting of Marian prayers, the *Salve Regina.* All over Europe the singing of the *Salve* each night after compline had become a popular devotion'.[6]

The Reformers criticised this antiphon – although Martin Luther wanted to retain it with one or two alterations.

> 'The English Reformers criticised the Hail Mary and similar forms of prayer, because they believed that it threatened the unique mediation of Jesus Christ' (para 67).[7]

However the Second Vatican Council endorsed the continued practice of believers asking Mary to pray for them, emphasising that "Mary's maternal role towards the human race in no way obscures or diminishes the unique mediation of Christ, but rather shows its power ... in no way does it hinder the direct union of believers with Christ, but rather fosters it" (para 60).[8]

It is also clear from the 2006 ARCIC Statement what the Anglican and Catholic members of the Commission have to say to the Reformers of the sixteenth century;

> 'The Scriptures invite Christians to ask their brothers and sisters to pray for them, in and through Christ (cf Jas 5:13-15). Those who are now 'with Christ', untrammelled by sin, share the unceasing prayer and praise which characterises the life of heaven, (eg Rev 5:9-14). Among all the saints, Mary takes her place as *Theotokos*: alive in Christ, she abides with the one she bore, still 'highly favoured' in the communion of grace and hope, the exemplar of redeemed humanity, an icon of the Church. Consequently she is believed to exercise a distinctive ministry of assisting others through her active prayer... Many experience a sense of empathy and solidarity with Mary, especially at key points when the account of her life echoes theirs, for example the acceptance of vocation, the scandal of her pregnancy, the improvised surroundings of her labour, giving birth, and fleeing as a refugee. Portrayals of Mary standing at the foot of the cross, and the traditional portrayal of her receiving the crucified body of Jesus (the *Pieta*), evoke the particular sufferings of a mother at the death of her child. Anglicans and Roman Catholics alike are drawn to the mother of Christ, as a figure of tenderness and compassion' (para 70, 71).[9]

Pre-eminent among the recorded apparitions of the Blessed Virgin Mary, listed in Appendix Three, is the events at Lourdes in southern France, close to the Pyrenees, in 1858. The young girl, Bernadette, who was much about the same age as Mary, when she experienced the visitation of the Archangel Gabriel, was a most unlikely recipient of divine favour; she had nothing going for her, but her poverty and innocence. Humanly speaking, Miriam of Nazareth too had little to recommend her, but the same qualities. But God's eye does not fall where humans look; He chose her to be the most important woman in human history.

The Peasant Girl of Lourdes

ST BERNADETTE (1844-1879)

There are certain parallels between Miriam of Nazareth and Marie Bernarde of Lourdes. Both came from poor families, living in small rural communities, one in the foothills of Galilee and the other in the foothills of the Pyrenees. Both were about fourteen years of age when, out of the blue, God made demands of them. Miriam was asked to be the mother of the Messiah and Marie Bernarde (affectionately known in her family as 'Bernadette') was asked by 'the Lady' who appeared to her (Miriam, Mother of God herself) to have a church built and encourage people to visit the site in pilgrimage. Miriam had difficulties in convincing people – particularly her betrothed, Joseph, – how she came to be pregnant. Bernadette had serious problems in convincing people that she really was seeing the Virgin Mary at the Massabielle Rock, by the river Gave.

The first apparition on 11 February 1858, while Bernadette was collecting driftwood from the river, took her completely by surprise; only she could see 'the Lady', as

Bernadette called her. Her local priest sent her packing when, on the Blessed Virgin's instructions, Bernadette told him of her visions. There were eighteen apparitions in all, and neither the parish priest nor the mayor, would accept the truth of what was happening, until the end. When Bernadette asked the Lady who she was, the reply was 'I am the Immaculate Conception' (a belief regarding Mary's sinless state only defined four years before by Pope IX). Bernadette was illiterate and there was absolutely no possibility that she would know about such a theological statement. Only when she persisted in visiting the parish priest and reported what the Blessed Virgin had said, did he believe her. A miraculous stream of water appeared at the foot of the Rock, and miraculous healings were reported. People began to flock to Lourdes, (nowadays, six million people a year visit the shrine).

Bernadette, who suffered from bad health all her life, remained composed as she was interrogated again and again. She shunned all publicity and was relieved when she was eventually allowed to join the Sisters of Notre Dame at Nevers, where she lived for the rest of her life. The remainder of her life (she died at the age of 35, in 1879) was one of suffering. Even in the convent, 300 miles from Lourdes, she was hounded by interrogations, pilgrims seeking her out and curious sightseers; all the while she endured a prolonged and painful illness with heroic fortitude and patience. Her body, buried in a damp grave for thirty years, was discovered to be incorrupt when it was exhumed in 1900 at the time of her beatification.

SUMMARY

Devotion to Mary, the Mother of Jesus, began in the Eastern Church, following the definition of the Council of Chalcedon (451) that she was to be honoured as *Theotokos*

(Mother of God). It spread and blossomed in Europe in the twelfth century. By the fifteenth century every church of any size had a Lady Chapel; England claimed for itself the title, 'Dowry of Mary'. The prayer, 'The Hail Mary', should give offence to no one. It divides into two halves; the first part is totally scriptural being two Bible texts from Luke's Gospel, run together. The second part uses the title 'Mother of God' from Chalcedon and simply asks her to pray for us. Anglican and Catholic theologians agree (ARCIC document) that 'The Scriptures lead us together to praise Mary as the handmaid of the Lord, who was providentially prepared by divine grace to be the mother of our Redeemer'.

NOTES – CHAPTER TEN

1. *The Stripping of the Altars* by Eamon Duffy, p.256.
2. *Made in the Marian Way;* an article in the Tablet, by Eamon Duffy.
3. *Already Within* by Daniel O'Leary, quoted in the Tablet.
4. *Mary, Grace and Hope in Christ* ARCIC document, p.28.
5. *Mary, Grace and Hope in Christ* ARCIC document, p.66.
6. *The Stripping of the Altars* by Eamon Duffy, p.264.
7. *Mary, Grace and Hope in Christ* ARCIC document, p.66.
8. The Second Vatican Council's Constitution on the Church, p.90.
9. *Mary, Grace and Hope in Christ* ARCIC document, p.70.

CHAPTER 11   *Focus:* STATUES OF THE SAINTS

THE COMMUNION OF SAINTS

Destruction by Puritans

No Catholic church would be complete without at least one statue or painting of a saint. Paintings of saints, and Biblical events, adorned the walls of all parish churches in England and Wales up to the Reformation; and it was the Puritans, in the 1640s, who went out of their way to destroy any statues or pictures that had survived. For them religious wall paintings, statues and even crosses were 'idolatrous relics of the old religion'. (The 'old religion' being Catholicism) Margaret Cavendish, Duchess of Newcastle, laments the excesses of Puritan beliefs and practices in her poem 'An antient Cross' first published in 1656:

> An antient Cross liv'd in our Fathers time,
> With as much Fame, as did the Worthyes nine;
> No harm it did, nor injury to none,
> But dwelt in peace, and quietly alone;
> Yet peaceful Nature, nor yet humble Minde,
> Shall not avoyd rude Ignorance that's blinde,
> That superstitiously beats down all things
> Which smell but of Antiquity, or springs
> From Noble Deeds, nor love, nor take delight,
> In Laws, or Justice, hating Truth and Right,
> But innovations love, for that seems fine,
> And what is new, adore they as divine;
> And so this Cross, poor Cross, all in a rage
> They pull'd down quite, the fault was onely Age.

The Cross referred to may have been the Cheapside Cross, erected in London at the end of the thirteenth century. It had niches containing statues of saints, apostles, bishops and Virgin and Child. So the Puritans, who demolished it on 2 May 1643, in their love of innovations, triumphed; but only for a short while. 'The Old Religion' returned to England and Wales and a part of its spirituality that is based on the Communion of Saints, is as vibrant as ever.

Communion of Saints

St Paul, in his letters, (e.g. Eph 1:15, 1:18, 6:18 and 1 Cor 6:2) refers to those who were faithful believers as 'saints'. (The word 'saints' is found some fifty times in the New Testament.) In the Apostolic age the Christians, who were referred to as 'saints', took seriously Paul's words, 'for he chose us in him before the creation of the world to be holy and blameless in his sight' (Eph 1:4). A natural consequence was that their profession of faith, the Apostles' Creed, crystallises these beliefs into 'the Communion of Saints'. The Second Vatican Council draws on several texts from Scripture to present the Church's teaching.

> 'When the Lord comes in glory, and all his angels with him, death will be no more and all things will be subject to him. But at the present time some of his disciples are pilgrims on earth. Others have died and are being purified while still others are in glory, contemplating 'in full light, God himself triune and one, exactly as he is' (para 49).[1]

Three Parts to the Communion

So there are three parts to the Communion of Saints:
(a) 'at present some of his disciples are pilgrims on earth';
(b) 'others have died and are being purified' (in purgatory);

(c) 'others are in glory'. These last are portrayed in the Book of Revelation (5:8) where it presents the saints interceding with God. It takes place in a dramatic scene, described by John the Evangelist, before the Lamb of God in heaven, when bowls of incense are offered, 'which are the prayers of the saints'; praying for those who are still disciples on earth.

The Apostles' Creed was probably written early in the second century (although a later date is proposed by some scholars). It has a list of twelve propositions for belief – the number probably indicates it's association with the Twelve Apostles. The ninth of these propositions is, 'I believe in the Communion of Saints'. This teaching is based primarily on 1 Corinthians 12:12, where Paul compares all baptised Christians to a single body. 'We were baptised' he writes, 'into one body in a single Spirit'.

Catholic teaching on the Communion of Saints – and by extension the beliefs and practices about 'saints' – is founded on the texts just quoted. Baptism, as we saw in chapter 7, is the essential gateway into membership of the Church. But this is not understood as just membership of the Institutional Church, or the local community, but of a Communion of all the baptised, in every age and place. The 'baptised' include those who have died and are with God in glory (this is called the Church Triumphant); the baptised who are still on life's journey (known as the Church Militant) and those Christians who have died, but are not yet with God in glory, delayed for purification in purgatory (the Church Penitent). So the doctrine of the Communion of Saints is that all the baptised ('the saints') are a single body, in which each member contributes to the good of all and shares in the welfare of all.

Prayers of the Saints

Catholics therefore believe – as the text from Revelation

(5:8) indicates – that the prayers of the saints can rise like incense before God and really assist those of the baptised who are still on their earthly pilgrimage. Equally the prayers of 'the saints' here on earth, in the Church Militant (still struggling with good and evil), can benefit the baptised, who have died, but have not yet attained union with God in glory. Hence the traditional Catholic practice of praying for the dead.

All the Baptised, wherever they are in the Communion of Saints, form one family. In ordinary families it is customary to have photographs on display of various family members, both living and dead. No one thinks it odd that grandparents, who are deceased, are still remembered with a photograph or two; nor that the uncle and aunt, who live in Australia, are remembered with a photograph. Likewise proud parents put up on the walls of their home, photos of sons and daughters in their mortar boards and graduation robes. This is what families do. And this is what the family of the Catholic Church does in having and displaying statues, paintings and mosaics of the saints, family members who have achieved the highest accolade; union with the Blessed Trinity in glory. We saw in chapter 3 how the Christians, who hid away in the catacombs, in the first two hundred years of the Church, chose the tombs of their heroes, those who had given their lives for Christ, as the place to celebrate the Eucharist. Those martyrs were considered saints, par excellence, and they were accorded respect and intercession was made to them. The practice has continued throughout the centuries:

> 'The story of saints in Britain stretches back to the earliest years of Christianity. An acquisitive age does not seem to have much regard for those who laboured for the Lord so many centuries ago, but their names remain and many are used in our day to day world. Some are so familiar that they pass unheeded from

the lips, Bart's (St Bartholomew's) and St Thomas's have no need to be called hospitals; St Leger has given his name to a horse race; and St Pancras is, as we all know, a railway station.'[2]

Patron Saints

Most of the over 9,000 Catholic and Anglican churches in England and Wales have patron saints (unless they are dedicated to Mary, the Mother of God.) Some 350 different saints are commemorated and 155 of these occur only once.

The idea of a church building having a special intercessor or advocate in heaven originated in Rome. Once the Emperor Constantine had, in 313 AD, granted freedom of worship to Christians, churches began to be built over the tombs of martyrs. Among the first were churches dedicated to St Callistus and St Sebastian, both on the Via Appia, near Rome. By the early Middle Ages the idea of having a saint as patron and special intercessor had spread to countries, places, trade guilds etc. until by the late Middle Ages virtually everything had a patron. So, St Cecilia became the patron of musicians, St George, the patron of soldiers, St Nicholas, patron of children and so on (see Appendix Six). Children, at baptism, received a 'Christian' name, which was always the name of a saint, who would be the child's special patron or intercessor in heaven. (Catholic families have attempted to hold on to this tradition, but with society's fascination with celebrities and the fashion for newly minted names, the tradition is almost lost.)

Intercession to the Saints

The Second Vatican Council had this to say about the Catholic tradition of intercession to the saints:

'The Church has always believed that the apostles, and Christ's martyrs who had given the supreme witness of faith and love by the shedding of their blood, are closely joined with us in Christ. She has always venerated them with special devotion, together with the Blessed Virgin Mary and the holy angels. The Church too has devoutly implored the aid of their intercession. To these were soon added those who had imitated Christ's virginity and poverty more exactly, and finally others whom the outstanding practice of the Christian virtues and the divine charisms recommended to the pious devotion and imitation of the faithful' (para 50).[3]

'It is not only by the title of example that we cherish the memory of those in Heaven. We do so still more in order that the union of the whole Church may be strengthened in the Spirit by the practice of fraternal charity (cf. Eph 4:1-6). For just as Christian communion among wayfarers brings us closer to Christ, so our companionship with the saints joins us to Christ, from whom as from their fountain and head issue every grace and the life of God's People itself' (para 50).[4]

Authentic practice

The Council wanted to make clear to Catholics the authentic way to honour the saints.

'Let the faithful be taught, therefore, that the authentic cult of the saints consists not so much in the multiplying of external acts, but rather in the intensity of our active love. By such love, for our own greater good and that of the Church, we seek from the saints example in their way of life, fellowship in their communion, and aid by their intercession. At the same time, let the people be instructed that our communion with those in heaven, provided that it is understood in the more adequate light of faith, in no way weakens, but conversely, more thoroughly enriches the supreme worship we give to God the Father, through Christ, in the Spirit' (para 51).[5]

The Agreed Statement of **ARCIC** on 'Mary, Grace and Hope in Christ' can provide us with the final word on the Communion of Saints.

'The Scriptures invite Christians to ask their brothers and sisters to pray for them, in and through Christ (cf. James 5:13-15). Those who are now "with Christ", untrammelled by sin, share the unceasing prayer and praise which characterises the life of heaven (e.g. Rev 5:9-14, 7:9-14). In the light of these testimonies, many Christians have found that requests for assistance in prayer can rightly and effectively be made to those members of the communion of saints distinguished by their holy living (cf. James 5:16-18). It is in this sense that we affirm that asking the saints to pray for us is not to be excluded as unscriptural, though it is not directly taught by the scriptures to be a required element of life in Christ' (para 70).[6]

The words 'example in their way of life', in the passage above from the Second Vatican Council's document on 'The Church', was taken very much to heart by Pope John Paul II. He believed that, in this ever secularising, materialist world in which we live today, Catholics need role models and saintly examples to inspire them. So he pursued the policy of acknowledging as many examples of heroic virtue and holiness as he could, by canonising a record number of saints.

The Saint-maker

POPE JOHN PAUL II (1920-2005)

Record number of canonisations

The American Atheist journal nicknamed Pope John Paul II 'the Saint-maker' in 2002. This was at the time of Padre Pio's canonisation, of which the magazine was very critical. The journal was cynical at the record number of 428 Catholics that the Pope had declared to be saints. This number of canonisations was, in fact, a very big increase and many more than the previous popes had 'raised to the altar'. Pope John Paul's policy must have reflected his personal belief, that those who had lived heroically spiritual lives and gained outstanding sanctity, should be recognised, and could provide Christian heroes for this Age to be inspired by and imitate.

The early martyrs

In the Church of the first few centuries, as we have seen in earlier chapters, it was the martyrs who were venerated by the faithful; canonisation (not that it was, in those days, called that) was by public acclaim. From the fourth century, the acknowledgement of 'sainthood' was extended to those who were called 'confessors'. These were Christians who had suffered for confessing their faith, but only to an extent which did not involve martyrdom. Later the term was applied loosely to markedly holy people, and ultimately those who were pronounced to be such by the Pope. The most famous example of this, in England, was King Edward the Confessor, who died in 1066; he was declared a saint by Pope Alexander III in 1161.

Proper process

The popes became involved, and a due process of canonisation was put in place, because negligence and abuses began to become widespread. (There were those who realised that there was much money to be made from such abuses; phoney claims, shrines etc.) The first recorded canonisation by a pope, John XV, in 993 was of St Ulrich of Augsburg. The long process by which an individual's sanctity was attested was made part of Church Law in the twelfth century. The process begins locally, at diocesan level and continues in Rome at the Congregation for the Causes of Saints. The evidence has to be scrutinised and tested at both levels. It is a lengthy process with various stages to go through, the most well known being 'Beatification'. This is an act by which the Pope permits the Catholic under investigation to be publicly venerated in certain parts of the Church. Pope John Paul II beatified 1,338 men and women, including the famous Albanian nun, Mother Teresa of Calcutta, in 2003.

No stranger to suffering

The cause of Pope John Paul's beatification is presently being considered and few have any doubts that he led a holy life, struggling, particularly in the last few years, courageously with illness. Karol Wojtyla was no stranger to suffering, it was part of his life from a very early age. His mother died just before his ninth birthday and his brother, Edmund, three years later. He was brought up by his father, an officer in the Austrian Army; he too died when Karol was 21. After the Nazi occupation of Poland he was forced, in slave conditions, to work as a stonecutter in a quarry.

Ordained at the age of 26, on 1 November 1946, he was sent to study in Rome. At the early age of 38 he was consecrated bishop and then began, as Bishop and eventually Archbishop of Cracow and Cardinal, a long struggle with the atheistic Communist government of Poland.

Elected Pope in 1978, John Paul made prayer and spirituality a central theme of his pontificate. He encouraged new religious movements, such as the Neo-Catechumenate, Communion and Liberation and Opus Dei. Around half a million members of these new movements gathered for the Pentecost Vigil in Rome in 1998. He inaugurated the World Youth Day in 1984 and met with gatherings of young people, every two years, in places like, Buenos Aires, Manila, and Cologne. Each occasion was attended by several million young people. His motivation was always to challenge the young people to deepen their spiritual lives and grow closer to Christ in prayer.

Pope John Paul's health was severely impaired as a result of the assassination attempt made on him on Wednesday, 13 May 1981. When he had recovered he visited his would-be assassin in prison in Rome, and forgave him.

Throughout the days of 1st and 2nd April 2005 the crowds that had flocked to St Peter's Square, Rome, at the news that the Pope was dying, publicly prayed and wept. John Paul II died on 2nd April, and immediately, worldwide calls were being made for him to be publicly acclaimed a saint. This appeal was resisted by the Church authorities, but on 13th May, the new Pope, Benedict XVI, announced that the cause for the beatification of John Paul II had been opened and that he had waived the usual rules which required a five-year wait before the Church begins to make investigations. Pope Benedict's announcement was made on the anniversary of the assassination attempt on Pope John Paul in 1981.

SUMMARY

Statues of saints in a Catholic church remind us of the ancient traditional belief in 'The Communion of Saints'. The Apostles' Creed (second century) is accepted by all Christian traditions; it includes the words, 'I believe in the Communion of Saints'.

Every human being who has been baptised – whether alive now, left this life and with God, or on their way to God (Purgatory) – are members of God's family. Paul uses the word 'saints' over 50 to describe the baptised, faithful members of the various Christian communities who 'are one body in a single Spirit'. Members of this one family can assist one another; the saints, the baptised with God in glory, can help us with their intercession to the Father. Anglican and Catholic theologians declared, 'we affirm that asking the saints to pray for us is not to be excluded as unscriptural.'[7]

NOTES – CHAPTER 11

1. The Second Vatican Council's Constitution on the Church, pp. 80 and 81.
2. *Discovering Saints in Britain* by John Vince, p.3.
3. The Second Vatican Council's Constitution on the Church, p.81.
4. The Second Vatican Council's Constitution on the Church, p.82.
5. The Second Vatican Council's Constitution on the Church, p.84.
6. *Mary, Grace and Hope in Christ* ARCIC document, p.69.
7. *Mary, Grace and Hope in Christ* ARCIC document, p.70.

CHAPTER 12   *Focus:* REPRESENTATION OF SACRED HEART

HEART OF LOVE

Symbol of the Heart

Most Catholic churches have, somewhere in the building, a statue or large picture of the Sacred Heart of Jesus; and there are a good number of parish churches in England and Wales dedicated to the Sacred Heart of Jesus. To the eye of a visitor, unfamiliar with the interior of a Catholic church, a statue or picture of the Sacred Heart of Jesus must appear rather peculiar. But, like the crucifix, it has to be viewed as a symbol of love. The heart, as a symbol of love, goes back into antiquity, long before the time of Christ. And in modern society much is made of the symbol of the heart in mid-February, associated with the legendary St Valentine. The annual celebration of Valentine's Day has become as well-established in Western society, and beyond, as Christmas Day. The fact that there is no historical link between St Valentine and protestations of human love, does not deter card and gift manufacturers. In contrast the very same, well-established, human symbol, used in a religious context, does have a theological, scriptural and spiritual link between the person of Jesus Christ and his love for humanity.

Scriptural foundations

Viewing the local Catholic church, as proposed in chapter one, as a time capsule, this devotion is the most modern, dating, in its present form, from the late eighteenth century. However, it is firmly founded on the immeasurable love of Christ, and Scripturally finds its foundation in the prayer of St Paul in his letter to the Christians of Ephesus:

> 'This, then is what I pray, kneeling before the Father, from whom every fatherhood, in heaven or on earth, takes its name. In the abundance of his glory may he, through his Spirit, enable you to grow firm in power with regard to your inner self, so that Christ may live in your hearts through faith, and planted in love and built on love, with all God's holy people you will have the strength to grasp the breadth and the length, the height and the depth; so that, knowing the love of Christ, which is beyond knowledge, you may be filled with the utter fullness of God.' (3:14-19)

This magnificent prayer not only provides, with the account in John 19:34 of the pierced side of Christ, the Biblical foundation for the devotion to the Sacred Heart of Jesus, but, beautifully, sums up the whole purpose of Catholic spirituality. Paul, the theologian and mystic, reveals the depth of his spirituality in this passage; 'knowing the love of Christ, which is beyond knowledge, you may be filled with the utter fullness of God'. (A Bible passage that could, with much benefit, be used for *Lectio Divina*, see chapter 5.)

The Medieval Mystics

It was the Mystics, particularly of the thirteenth and fourteenth centuries, who, through their contemplative writings, introduced, under the guidance of the Holy Spirit, a devout pondering on the immeasurable love of Christ. For them it was associated with the wound in the side of Christ, as he hung upon the cross. The **Franciscan** Order (as we saw in chapter 9) preached around Europe, devotion to the crucified form of Christ on the cross and his five wounds. The Franciscan theologian, St Bonaventure (1217-

1274), who was accorded the title 'Doctor Seraphicus', was the first to write, in his books, *Vitis mystica* and *De lingo vitae*, of a connection between the wound in Christ's side, his wounded heart, and the immeasurable love of Jesus. We shall never know whether the mystics, St Mechtild of Hackeborn (d.1299), and St Gertrude (d.1302), had read Bonaventure's books or not, but both had well documented visions that confirmed them in their own devotion to the Sacred Heart of Jesus. However the devotion was long confined to a relatively small number of mystics and saints. These included, in England, Julian of Norwich and in Italy, St Frances of Rome.

Theological developments

In the sixteenth century the devotion was extended and fostered by the **Carthusians** and, a little later, by the **Jesuits**. St Francis de Sales (see page 71) imbued his religious congregation, the Visitation Sisters, with an ardent devotion of the Sacred Heart of Jesus and, alongside the Jesuits, they worked to secure a place in the official, as well as the popular, life of the Church. The first theologian to work out the theological and liturgical foundations for private devotion and press for the celebration of a public feast day was St John Eudes (1601-1680).

Visions of St Margaret Mary

However it was not until St Margaret Mary Alacoque, a Visitation Sister, had visions of the Sacred Heart of Jesus, and the controversy that raged around these, that the Catholic faithful began to take note.

In December 1673, Margaret Mary recorded the following words that she reported had been addressed to her by Christ during a revelation:

> 'My Divine Heart is so passionately inflamed with love… that, not being able any longer to contain within itself the flames of its ardent love, it must let them spread abroad through your means, and manifest itself to humanity, that they may be enriched with its precious treasures which I unfold to you, and which contain the sanctifying and salutary graces that are necessary to hold them back from the abyss of ruin.'

The content of the revelations gave a definite shape to the object of devotion and its practices. Its most prominent feature was reparation for the outrages committed against the Blessed Sacrament. It was not until 1765, seventy-five years after St Margaret Mary's death, that official approval was given by Pope Clement XIII to devotion to the Sacred Heart of Jesus. In 1856 Pope Pius IX extended the feast of the Sacred Heart to the whole universal Church and, in 1899, Leo XIII consecrated all humankind to the Sacred Heart of Jesus. The annual feast day is observed on the Friday in the week after **Corpus Christi**.

Teaching Letter of Pope Pius XII

In 1956 Pope Pius XII published an encyclical letter dedicated to the Devotion to the Sacred Heart of Jesus. In it he carefully outlines the Scriptural and historical background, recommending the devotion to the whole Church. Then he concludes with this point:

> Today, more than at any other time, we see individuals, families, nations, the whole world attacked and undermined by innumerable evils. Where can we seek a remedy? Could we find a more excellent way, and one which accords with the essential spirit of the Catholic Faith, than a devotion

which is totally directed towards the very love of God Himself?' (para 69).[1]

Pope Benedict XVI's first letter

The first encyclical letter of Pope Benedict XVI was called 'God is Love' and the Pope has this to say:

> 'Christ's death on the cross is the culmination of that turning of God against himself in which he gives himself in order to raise man up and save him. This is love in its most radical form. By contemplating the pierced side of Christ (cf. Jn 19:37), we can understand the starting point of this letter: "God is love". It is there that this truth can be contemplated. It is from there that our definition of love must begin. In this contemplation the Christian discovers the path along which his life and love must move' (para 12).[2]

The Pope does not use the words, 'the Sacred Heart of Jesus', but the thought and theology is the same; his letter acts as an interpretation.

Popular Devotion in England and Wales

Devotion to the Sacred Heart of Jesus was very popular, throughout Europe, before the Second Vatican Council. It took the form of families having their homes consecrated to the Sacred Heart and individuals making the **First Nine Fridays**.

One example of the strength of devotion to the Sacred Heart of Jesus, in England and Wales, in the nineteenth and first half of the twentieth century was the existence of several **Confraternities** that promoted it. One such confraternity was centred upon the Visitation Sisters'

Convent at Roselands, Walmer, Kent (demolished in the 1970s). The Confraternity was called 'The Guard of Honour of the Sacred Heart of Jesus'; it was approved by Pope Leo XIII in 1875 and within ten years it had 250,000 members, enrolled in over 900 approved centres. Members of the Confraternity inspired by the words of Psalm 69, 'scorn has broken my heart and has left me helpless; I look for sympathy, and found none', pledge to give time each day, in a round-the-clock programme of adoration. The object of the Confraternity is laid out in its handbook:

> 'To render a perpetual and uninterrupted worship of Glory, Love and Reparation to the most Sacred Heart of Jesus, once visibly wounded with the lance on the tree of the Cross, and now invisibly wounded every day by scorn, forgetfulness, and ingratitude. To accomplish this end, the associates choose one hour in the day, called the *Hour of Guard* during which, without changing any of their ordinary occupations, they endeavour, in a more special manner, to glorify, to love and to console the Sacred Heart of Jesus.'[3]

There follows, in the Handbook, prayers and suggested ways of fulfilling the pledge of one hour of adoration and praise.

While the Confraternity does not appear to exist any longer in the United Kingdom it is still promoted by some Visitation convents around the world, notably in Krakow, Poland and in Alabama, USA. Following the Second Vatican Council devotion to the Sacred Heart of Jesus waned considerably, due to a greater emphasis upon lay involvement in the liturgy, the weekly reception of Holy Communion and the decline in evening services, like Benediction. However some parish communities have retained the devotional practice of having a special Mass on the first Friday of each month.

Apart from St Margaret Mary, and the powerful influence of her visions, no one did more in the seventeenth century to promote Devotion to the Sacred Heart of Jesus than John Eudes.

The Plague Priest

ST JOHN EUDES (1601-1680)

The normal human reaction to the dangers of contamination is to avoid all possible contact with the source of the infection. This is particularly true if the danger is life threatening. John Eudes went deliberately into plague infested areas of Normandy in 1627 and again in 1631, with no thought for himself, to nurse and bring spiritual comfort to the dying. Born at Ri, Normandy, and educated at the Jesuit college at Caen, John joined the Oratorians (Congregation of the Oratory) and was ordained in 1625. He conducted missions around France for ten years and then, in 1641, in the course of his work, he became aware of the need to help prostitutes who wanted to break away from their old lives. With Madeleine Lamy he founded a refuge for them. This was placed under the direction of the Visitation Order, that had been founded by St Francis de Sales. John had a deep devotion to the Sacred Heart of Jesus and promoted it continually through his Mission and Retreat work. In 1643 he withdrew from the Oratory and founded, at Caen, the Congregation of Jesus and Mary, which was an association of secular priests, dedicated to the Sacred Heart. The Eudists (as they were called) concentrated on upgrading the standard of the clergy by establishing effective seminaries and preaching missions.

His foundation was opposed by the Oratorians and the Jansenists, and he was unable to get Papal approval for it, but in 1650, the Bishop of Coutances invited him to establish a seminary in his diocese. The same year the sisters, working at his refuge in Caen, left the Visitation Order and were recognised by the Bishop of Bayeux as a new Congregation called the Sisters of Our Lady of Charity of the Refuge.

John founded seminaries throughout Normandy and continued for the rest of his life giving missions and promoting devotion to the Sacred Heart of Jesus. He shared with St Margaret Mary Alacoque the honour of initiating this devotion; writing books and composing a Mass to the Sacred Heart in 1668. He died at Caen, on 19 August 1680, which day, after his canonisation in 1925, became his feast day.

SUMMARY

The human symbol for love, the heart, as portrayed in statues and pictures of the Sacred Heart of Jesus reminds us of the immeasurable love of Christ, who was both human and divine. First, the writings of the Medieval Mystics, then the revelations made to St Margaret Mary Alacoque directed Catholic thoughts to the immeasurable (Eph 3:14) love of Christ for humanity. The resulting devotion to the symbol of the human heart of Christ, filled with divine love, became very helpful and popular in the eighteenth to nineteenth centuries.

NOTES – CHAPTER 12

1. *Haurietis Aquas* Encyclical Letter of Pope Pius XII (CTS booklet), p.44.
2. *Deus Caritas Est* by Pope Benedict XVI, p.16.
3. *Handbook of the Hour of Guard* Confraternity of the Guard of Honour, p.8.

CHAPTER 13   *Focus:* SEASONAL COLOURS

THE LITURGICAL YEAR

Changing colours

What will not be evident straightaway, to a visitor to a Catholic church, is that the colour of the outer vestments worn by the priest and the coverings, or hangings, on the altar and around the sanctuary, change according to the season in the Liturgical calendar. While the use of different colours, for example, purple for Lent and white for Christmas, help the recollection of worshippers and add to the dignity of the celebration, they are not essential. The use of colours in connection with worship has a varied history and certainly did not exist for the first thousand years of Catholicism. For that period of time the colour of the priestly vestments, and the hangings, was without liturgical significance, save for a preference for white robes. The garments that were customarily worn among the Roman middle and upper classes in the Empire, and in its Byzantine continuation, continued to be used into the Middle Ages. The indications are that the clergy reserved a special 'suit' of civilian dress, consisting of an alb (from the Latin 'albus' meaning 'white') and chasuble for use in church on Sundays and feast days. It is not until the twelfth century that a correlation started to be made between significant colours and the seasonal feasts of the Church's Year.

Liturgical colours evolve

It is surprising to know that the Augustinian **Canons** at Jerusalem, in the twelfth century, were the first to work out a sequence of colours, and they chose black for Christmas! That selection did not catch on and, with the passing of time, the increase in wealth in European society encouraged more lavish vestments and the use of a wider range of colours and variety of textiles. Different areas of the Church made their own choices. Gradually, however, a generally accepted pattern of colour association emerged, but a general rule was not formally defined until 1570 in the reformed Roman Missal of Pope Pius V.

Colours explained

In brief, the colours prescribed are – white (for purity and joy) used for the feasts of Christ, like Christmas and Easter; red (for fire and blood) for Pentecost, the feast days of the Apostles, and the martyrs; green (for life and growth) used for the ordinary Sundays of the year; purple (for sorrow and repentance) is used for the Sundays, and week days, of Advent and Lent. Purple is also worn for funerals, although nowadays white, which is always used for the funerals of children, is sometimes chosen. Black was originally approved for funerals, but since the Second Vatican Council it has been replaced with purple.

The Liturgical Year

The Liturgical Year is not just a structure for organising the Church's public worship, it has a theological meaning, which is central to Catholic Spirituality. In reforming the Liturgy the Second Vatican Council went back to basics.

> 'Holy Mother Church is conscious that she must celebrate the saving work of her divine Spouse by devoutly recalling it on certain days throughout the course of the year. Every week, on the day which she has called the Lord's day, she keeps the memory

of His resurrection. In the supreme solemnity of Easter she also makes an annual commemoration of the resurrection, along with the Lord's blessed passion. Within the cycle of a year, moreover, she unfolds the whole mystery of Christ, not only from His incarnation and birth until His ascension, but also as reflected in the day of Pentecost, and expectation of a blessed, hoped-for return of the Lord' (para 102).[1]

Easter every week

So each week the Resurrection of Christ is celebrated on Sunday, and the central focus and highlight of the year is the celebration of Easter. The Death and Resurrection of Christ is central to Catholic Spiritual life and worship. Salvation for the individual, not alone, but as a member of the community of the Risen Christ, is integral to the work and love relationships within the life of the Holy Trinity.

> 'The purpose of the whole salvific order, as seen by God, is that everything created is meant to be reconciled to the Father through the working of his Son, through the divinising power of his Spirit. The redeeming work of the crucified and risen Jesus consists in giving us his Spirit of love through whom we may know the Father and the fullness of the Son (Jn 17:3) and thus we ourselves, by the power of the Holy Spirit, can become truly children of God.'[2]

Sunday, as the first day of the week, on which day Christ rose from the dead, takes precedence over all other feasts and festivals, apart from feasts of the Lord, like Christmas Day.

Observing the Lord's Day

Catholics do not, strictly speaking, observe the third of the Ten Commandments, 'Remember to keep holy the Sabbath Day', because the Sabbath is Saturday; and that is the Jewish holy day. The difference in practice is neatly observed in the old City of Jerusalem, where in the Arab Quarter all the shops are closed on Friday (the Muslim holy day); while round the corner in the Jewish and Christian areas all the shops are open. But on Saturday (the Sabbath) the Jewish shops are all boarded up, while trading continues in the other areas; and the same happens on a Sunday in the Christian Quarter.

Commercial Christmas v. Christian Christmas

Modern Society makes much of Christmas; some would say, too much! In a capitalist world dominated by consumerism it is inevitable that the commercial opportunity presented by the tradition of gift-giving would not be missed! The modern commercialised winter festival has little to do with the Christmas of the liturgical calendar. The Church's Year does give importance to Christmas, but not the first importance. Catholics are not, or should not be, 'Christmas Christians'; but 'Easter Christians', whose song is 'Alleluia'! It is thought provoking to know and understand that Christmas was not celebrated in the Christian Church during the first three centuries; many millions of Christians lived and died without ever hearing of or celebrating Christmas! Easter was everything to them; all else paled before it. The very first recorded celebration of Christmas Day (not the season) was in the early fourth century, probably in 336, in Rome. It took another century for the practice to spread throughout northern Europe.

Easter Vigil – central event of the Catholic Year

The most important celebration of the Catholic liturgical year is the Easter Vigil, which is celebrated, after dark, on the evening of Holy Saturday. (Often misnamed and identified in secular society as 'Easter Saturday'. Naturally this is the Saturday after Easter, not before it has occurred!) The whole community of the local parish should be gathered in their church, awaiting the lighting of the new fire, which represents, with the Easter Candle the Risen Christ. (Sadly, not all Catholics understand and appreciate the importance and centrality of the Easter Vigil and do not take part.) The tall, especially and symbolically decorated, Easter Candle is dramatically borne on high into the church, where the people are waiting its arrival in the dark. Gradually, and symbolically, the light spreads throughout the church as people light their individual candles from the Easter Candle. The Vigil service, that follows, is full of symbolism, centred around the symbols of fire and water, as the Resurrection is celebrated. It is at this service that new converts (called catechumens) to Catholicism are baptised and received into the community.

Season of Lent

This brings us to the season of Lent during which, in earlier times, the catechumens would make their final preparation for Easter. Named, in the English-speaking world, after the old English word Lenten for 'Spring', Lent is the penitential period of forty days before Easter. Nowadays, it is not so strictly kept as in the past. In the early centuries, it was a time of very strict fasting for the whole community, not just the catechumens. Only one meal a day was allowed, with an abstinence from meat and fish included. The length of the period of 'forty days' was suggested by the 40 days' fast of Moses (Exod 24:18),

Elijah (1 Kings 14:8) and especially of the Lord himself, in the wilderness after his baptism by John the Baptiser (Mt 4:2).

Observing Lent

While fasting, and abstinence from meat, is now only mandatory on two days of Lent, **Ash Wednesday** and **Good Friday**, most modern Catholics, who take their spiritual life seriously, try to make good use of the opportunities presented by the season. This could be by abstaining from something pleasurable (hence the old phrase, 'giving up something for Lent'), for example, giving up a favourite TV programme; or, more positively it might be by engaging in something extra, for example, going to morning Mass during the week or services of the Way of the Cross (also called Stations of the Cross). Traditionally, the purpose of Lent has been summarised by the three words; repentance, almsgiving and prayer.

> It is a time – for a change of heart. A time for a new and closer look at the way our lives are lived, for repentance and reconciliation.
>
> It is a time – for concern for others. Caring for others is a valuable weapon in our fight against selfishness. Almsgiving has always been a part of Lent.
>
> It is a time – for prayer which costs. That means in terms of time and personal effort.[3]

Holy Week

Lent concludes with **Holy Week**. This is the week, which starts with Passion Sunday (still popularly known as 'Palm Sunday', because palms are blessed and distributed on that day) and includes Maundy Thursday, Good Friday and

Holy Saturday/Easter Sunday. These three, the most sacred days of the Christian year, are called 'The Easter Triduum'. It works out as three (although it appears to be four days) because the 'days' are counted from evening to evening, which follows the Jewish practice. In this way; the first 'day' is from Maundy Thursday evening (during which the memorial meal of Christ's Last Supper is celebrated; and his death on the cross) to Good Friday evening. The second day is from Good Friday evening to Saturday evening (during which the burial and 'silence' of the grave is recalled.) The third day is from Saturday evening to Easter Sunday evening, during which, at the Easter Vigil and Sunday morning Masses the glorious Resurrection of Christ is celebrated.

Season of Advent

As Christmas began to be celebrated throughout Europe, in the fifth century, the question arose, should it, like Easter, be preceded by a season of preparation?

In the late sixth century the practice was established of a period of four weeks of preparation, including four Sundays, called 'Advent'. The title comes from the Latin word *Adventus*, meaning 'Coming'. It was to be similar to Lent, as a period of penitence and abstinence, but the fasting was not to be so strict. The penitential character of the season was, and still is, marked by the use of purple vestments and hangings and simplicity in the subdued use of music and floral arrangements.

Waiting for the Coming

The emphasis, in the Scripture readings and prayers, during this season is upon waiting for the coming. By 'the coming' (Advent) is meant the coming of Christ; as the Second

Person of the Holy Trinity born a human child; as the teacher who is going to impart the Good News of the Kingdom; and finally, as the Judge at the end of time (also called 'the Final Coming'). Even some regular churchgoers are a little surprised to find John the Baptist – heralding Christ's coming as a teacher – figuring in the Bible texts. And the same is true of the readings that speak of the final coming of Christ. The virtues proposed during this season are patience, faithfulness and humility. All of this is in stark contrast to the brash, glittery world of the secular commercialism that runs riot from late October to 24 December.

Preparing for, not pre-empting

The Catholic liturgy promotes the idea that there is virtue in acknowledging our need of the redemption that the Christ Child brought, and as generations before Christ waited patiently for God to reveal himself, so should we experience a little of that patience in our waiting for his Coming. This 'waiting' can enrich Christmas, when it comes. All the decorations, gifts and carols, can 'burst', in rapturous joy on the liturgical scene on Christmas Eve, at the first Mass of Christmas. Pre-empting the festival, with, for example, carols sung weeks before Christmas Day, destroys the whole concept of Advent. The commercial, materialistic 'Christmas' begins in late October and ends on Christmas Eve – when the New Year Sales notices go up. The Catholic Christmas begins at the end of Advent, on Christmas Eve, and continues to the feast of the Epiphany and the visit of the Magi (Three Kings) on 6 January and the twelfth day of Christmas (see Appendix Five).

The liturgical year exists for the praise and glory of God, pre-eminently through the Easter mysteries, and for the development and formation of the spiritual lives of Catholics.

'In the various seasons of the year and according to her traditional discipline, the Church completes the formation of the faithful by means of pious practices for soul and body, by instruction, prayer, and works of penance and charity' (para 105).[4]

The saint most closely associated with the Liturgical year is, at the same time, extremely popular, and unrecognised by most people, as a saint. Flashing replicas inhabit rooftops and bouncing inflatable models abound in gardens; human versions bestow gifts in stores and seasonal fayres. Santa Claus is everywhere during Advent and the Christmas season. Few people appreciate that they are perpetuating and celebrating the traditions associated with St Nicholas, patron saint of children and of Russia.

Santa Claus

ST NICHOLAS (d.c.350)

Some Christian families have a problem about Santa Claus, or Father Christmas. They feel there is a conflict between the real meaning of Christmas and the Father Christmas myth. This should not be a problem for Catholic families with the background of a traditional reverence and respect for the saints. 'Santa Claus' is a name which has been broken down through regular usage from 'Sinter Claes', which is the Dutch for Saint Nicholas. The name has entered into the English language and culture through the Dutch settlers who went and set up home in North America.

Saint Nicholas lived around the fourth century and was probably the bishop of Myra, in Asia Minor, (a town which nowadays would be in modern Turkey). His existence is only known of through traditional stories. It seems that after being born in Asia Minor he travelled widely and eventually suffered imprisonment for his Christian faith under the Emperor Diocletian. (Parts of his story have, over the centuries, been combined with that of his namesake, Nicholas Sionites.) He was famous – so tradition has it – for his loving concern of the needy and especially for children and young people. There are many legends of St Nicholas, lovingly preserved in the Russian Orthodox Church; he is the patron of Russia and the subject of many icons. All the stories tell of his generosity, and include, saving seafarers; saving a boy from drowning; rescuing a kidnapped child; saving three falsely accused town councillors; but the best known one is of the three poor marriageable young girls. (Different versions of this story have come down to us.) A poor widow, whose rich husband had lost all his wealth, and his life, left her with three daughters. The eldest was of marriageable age but could not marry because her widowed mother was too poor to provide a dowry. The legend goes that, hearing of their plight, Bishop Nicholas secretly, in the middle of the night, left a bag of gold coins at their house. Not long afterwards she found a husband. Time passed and the second daughter became marriageable; Bishop Nicholas repeated his kindness. When some time later the third daughter became marriageable Nicholas crept by a third time, but this time, as he left the money, he was caught sight of by the mother. The traditional story ends with the mother throwing herself at the feet of the saint, thanking him for his generosity.

This story is obviously the basis of the Santa Claus, delivering gifts in the middle of the night, tradition. This practice was imitated, on 6 December, in New Amsterdam (New York) where the Dutch settlers lived; it was they who developed the traditional story into the form we have now; and exported it to England.

The Russian Orthodox Church has innumerable churches dedicated to him and retains many stories of miracle icons of St Nicholas. Devotion to the saint had arrived in the West by 1087, when records show there were, in England, thirteen churches dedicated to him. His intercession was sought, especially by merchants and seafarers and so churches dedicated to him are found in or near to ports, for example the twelfth-century church of St Nicholas at Great Wakering, Essex, was built close to a former port at North Shoebury. St Nicholas' feast day is 6th December, a former date for Christmas in Holland.

SUMMARY

The use of liturgical colours is helpful, but not essential; they do not have a scriptural or theological background or a long history. What is absolutely essential, in the Church's liturgical year, is the annual celebration of the death and resurrection of the Lord at Easter, and in particular the rituals of the Easter Vigil. The weekly celebration of Easter, on the Lord's Day, is also important and it takes precedence over all other festivals (except those of Christ) and celebrations. While Lent, the season of preparation for Easter, is of ancient origin, Advent, as the season of preparation for Christmas, is more recent.

NOTES – CHAPTER 13

1. The Second Vatican Council's Constitution on the Liturgy, pp.167-168.
2. *Prayer of the Heart* by George Maloney SJ, p.72.
3. *Let's Celebrate* by Tony Castle, p.45.
4. The Second Vatican Council's Constitution on the Liturgy, pp.169.

Focus: THE DIVINE MERCY

DEVELOPMENTS IN CATHOLIC SPIRITUALITY

Pictures of the Divine Mercy

Occasionally, in church, may be seen a picture or poster of what is called 'The Divine Mercy'. This is a striking variant on the portrayal of the Sacred Heart of Jesus. While there are slightly different depictions – the Apostles' Image; the Hyla Image; Skemp Image etc – they all have in common the picture of a manly figure of Christ, dressed in white, with his right hand raised in blessing and, strikingly, two large rays of light, one red the other pale yellow streaming from Christ's chest. Under the painted figure are always printed the words, 'Jesus I trust in you'. The original, life-size image, which is called the 'Vilnius image' was painted at the direction of the twentieth-century visionary, St Maria Faustina.

Movements in Spirituality

Trends and movements in Catholic spirituality come and go. Some cause a great stir and attract a large following for a while, but, in time, fade away. Other devotional practices mature, under the guidance of the Holy Spirit, and become absorbed into the life of the Church. (We have already encountered several of these, for example, the devotional use of the Stations of the Cross and the Rosary.)

Liturgy comes first

In some cultures, for example, in South America, where numerically most Catholics live, popular devotional life some times tends to be a fascinating mix of traditional pre-Christian beliefs with the more visual and emotional elements of Catholicism. (This is particularly true in Holy Week with the public dramatisations of the Passion of Christ.) The Second Vatican Council may have had these in mind when it declared,

> 'Popular devotions of the Christian people are warmly commended, provided they accord with the laws and norms of the Church... these devotions should be so drawn up that they harmonise with the liturgical seasons, accord with the sacred liturgy, are in some fashion derived from it, and lead people to it, since the liturgy by its very nature far surpasses any of them' (para 13).[1]

Examples of developments

Four examples follow of developments in Spirituality that started well before the twentieth century, and were very helpful to many Catholics for the first half of last century, but, while they still exist, to some degree, in the life of the Church, they no longer retain the same interest and following.

In chapter 12 we explored the Devotion to the Sacred Heart of Jesus and traced its origins, particularly as a result of the visionary experiences of St Margaret Mary Alacoque in the 1670s. As we saw, in the 1940s and 1950s, devotion to the Sacred Heart of Jesus was extremely, universally popular. It declined steadily after the Second Vatican Council and although it still exists, there are no longer any special weekly services, annual processions or pilgrimages.

The Children of Mary

Another very popular devotional aid that had a huge following in the years prior to the Second Vatican Council was the Miraculous Medal. In many parishes there were weekly evening services, based upon this devotion; there were pilgrimages and a sodality for women called 'The Children of Mary'. This parish-based women's group would meet weekly, recite the rosary and organise charitable and social events. On public occasions, for example, the May outdoor Procession, in honour of the Blessed Virgin, the Children of Mary members wore blue smock-like cloaks and white head veils.

The Miraculous Medal

The Miraculous Medal owes its origin to Zoe Labore, a member of the Daughters of Charity of St Vincent de Paul, who, as a religious, had the name Sr Catherine. While still a novice, in the Mother-house of the Religious Congregation on the Rue de Bac, in Paris, in 1830, Catherine experienced visions of the Blessed Virgin Mary. There were three apparitions in the chapel, while Catherine was at prayer. Mary appeared to her sitting on a chair in the sanctuary. She asked Catherine to have a medal struck to honour her Immaculate Conception (defined as Church doctrine in 1854). The medal was to be oval in shape, on one side designed with an image of Mary, with outstretched arms, with the words, 'O Mary, conceived without sin, pray for us who have recourse to thee'. On the reverse side, the letter M with a cross and twelve stars above it and the hearts of Jesus and Mary.

Claims of miracles

The large number of miracles, that were claimed to have happened in response to the prayers of those wearing this medal, gave rise to it being called 'Miraculous'. Catherine had the usual problems of visionaries of not being believed or her visions accepted. However, two years later, 1832, the first fifteen hundred, of what were to be eventually tens-of-millions, were minted. The apparitions of the Virgin Mary were approved as authentic in 1836, after lengthy investigations by a special Church commission. Catherine Laboure (1806-1876) lived a very humble life and was canonised as a saint by Pope Pius XII in 1947.

The Legion of Mary

Founded in 1921, in Dublin, by Frank Duff, the Legion of Mary was a familiar and popular association of lay people found, before the Second Vatican Council, in most Catholic parishes. Duff modelled his sodality, dedicated to the service of Christ, through a devotion to the Virgin Mary, on the Roman Army and used the titles, like *praesidium*, *curia* and *senatus*, to distinguish the different levels of the organisation. The founder's stated intention was 'to help Catholic lay people fulfil their baptismal promises and be able to live their dedication to Jesus Christ and the Church in an organised structure, supported by fellowship and prayer'. The spirituality of the Legion is this 'total dedication' to Christ through devotion to the Virgin Mary.

When it was first founded the Legion met with mistrust, as it engaged in parish work, like visiting the sick; the 'lay apostolate', as it was called, was unfamiliar to Catholics in the 1920s. It was only after a commendation by Pope Pius XI, in 1931, that the Legion began to be accepted. It was an inspiration to many and did much good in ordinary parish life throughout the '40s and '50s.

The promotion and encouragement of lay involvement in the life of the Church by the Second Vatican Council (especially the Decree on the Laity) meant that a Catholic did not need to belong to an association to assist in parish life. This was one of the reasons why the Legion of Mary's presence in parishes declined in the years following the Council.

Green Scapular Devotion

As a result of an apparition of the Virgin Mary to Sr Justine Bisqueburu, in Paris, France, on 28 January 1840, (eventually approved and supported by Pope Pius IX) the Green **Scapular** was launched. Sr Justine was, like St Catherine Labore, a member of the Congregation of the Daughters of Charity, and she had the same **Spiritual Director**, Fr Aladel. According to Sr Justine, Our Lady asked her to have scapulars made that would have a picture of her on one side; a heart pierced by a sword circled by the words 'Immaculate Heart of Mary, pray for us now and at the hour of our death' on the reverse side. Wearers were encouraged to say the prayer on the scapular regularly and they were assured of the prayers of the Virgin Mary that they would be kept from evil and benefit from a holy death.

The Green Scapular enjoyed great popularity in the 1940s and '50s and there are still Catholic associations, for example, The Apostolate of the Green Scapular of Houston, USA, that promote it, but generally it is unknown to most twenty-first-century Catholics.

New 'Devotions' replace old

As with Devotion to the Sacred Heart of Jesus and the Legion of Mary, the devotional practices associated with the Miraculous Medal and the Green Scapular have declined steadily since the mid-1960s. However there have in recent years been new developments in Catholic Spirituality, in addition to those directly promoted by the liturgical reforms of the Second Vatican Council (see Appendix Four).

Charismatic Renewal Movement

As understanding of the reforms of the Second Vatican Council grew, a new development took place in Catholic

Spirituality in Europe. Starting in North America, in the late '60s, there was a revival of Pentecostalism in many Christian churches, which spread into the Catholic Church, where it was called the Charismatic Renewal Movement. (*Charisma* is the Greek for 'gifts'.) It was encouraged by the inspirational writing of Cardinal Leo Suenans, particularly his *A New Pentecost*. The Movement was characterised by much enthusiasm, and the 'gifts' of speaking in tongues, spiritual healing, fainting in the Spirit, etc. One of the benefits, to the whole Catholic Church, of this short-lived expression of Spirituality, was the re-awakening and deeper appreciation of the role of the Holy Spirit in the life of the Church. Since 1987, and the Rome Synod of Bishops on the Laity, the Movement has been officially recognised, more structured and become theologically more restrained and conservative.

Celtic Spirituality

In recent years a great deal of interest has been shown, not only in the Catholic Church, but also in the Anglican Communion and across the Christian traditions, in the spirituality of the early Celtic Church. Naturally Irish writers and spiritual guides, like John O'Donohue, with his books *Anam Cara* and *Eternal Echoes*, have been foremost in this movement.

Creation Spirituality

Closely linked to the development of interest in Celtic Spirituality has been the work of theologians and spiritual writers, (and the great Catholic scientist and mystic Teilhard de Chardin) who have examined Scripture and Theology in the light of scientific work on ecology and environmental studies. Outstanding among these theologians has been

Sean McDonagh, with his seminal books, *To Care for the Earth* (1987) and *The Greening of the Church* (1990). The resulting 'Creation Spirituality' is an exciting new development, which, sadly, we have no space to consider in this 'Introduction'.

In the last decade, devotion based upon the Divine Mercy, encouraged by the support of Pope John Paul II, has become popular among many Catholics. It is founded upon the religious experiences of St Maria Faustina.

Visionary of the Divine Mercy

ST MARIA FAUSTINA (1905-1938)

Humble beginnings

Helena Kowalska was the third of ten children from a very poor family. At the age of fifteen, having only received three years of education, she was forced to work to help support her family. Her poor education resulted in her being turned away from various convents in Warsaw, Poland, when she sought to follow her vocation and gain admittance to the religious life. She was finally accepted at the convent of the Congregation of the Sisters of Our Lady of Mercy. In April 1926, at the age of 21, she took her first vows and the name in religion of Sr Maria Faustina of the Blessed Sacrament. (The practice of retaining your baptismal name when entering the religious life was restored by the Second Vatican Council in the late 1960s.)

The visions of Divine Mercy

Sister Faustina, as she is known today, began to experience visions and claimed to have spoken to Jesus and Mary several times; and even to have visited Purgatory. Jesus, Faustina claimed, revealed his purpose, which was to alert people to the mercy of God and spread devotion to the mercy of God. On 22 February 1931, Jesus was reported to have appeared as the 'King of Divine Mercy'; he was wearing a white garment, his right hand raised in blessing and, where his left hand touched his breast, two large bright rays, red and pale yellow, emanated. With the help of her confessor and spiritual director, Fr Michal Sopocko, Sr Faustina had a picture of the vision painted; copies were circulated and people began to use them for private devotion. Despite her limited literacy Faustina began to keep a diary of her visions and what was said to her in them. The diary was later published as *Divine Mercy in My Soul: The Diary of St Faustina*. She tried to found a congregation to proclaim the mercy of God to the world, but her convent refused her permission to do so.

Content of the Revelations

During the course of the revelations received by Sr Faustina Christ asked that a feast day, dedicated to the Divine Mercy should be celebrated, and this should be on the Sunday after Easter (the second Sunday of Easter). This special day was first kept in Poland and then, by a decree dated 23 May 2000, it was extended to the Universal Church. The Decree stated that, 'throughout the world the Second Sunday of Easter will receive the name Divine Mercy Sunday, a perennial invitation to the Christian world to face, with confidence in divine benevolence, the difficulties and trials that mankind will experience in the years to come'.

Sick and suffering

In 1936, Sr Faustina became extremely ill with tuberculosis and she was moved to a sanatorium in Pradnik, where she spent much time in prayer for the conversion of sinners. She suffered greatly and in June 1938 could no longer write her diary; she died on 5th October. While very sick she had furthered her mission to spread the word that people should place their entire trust in the wonderful mercy of God; her work was continued after her death by her spiritual director, Fr Sopocko, who never doubted the authenticity of her mystical experiences. The religious community that Sr Faustina had dreamed of founding 'The Institute of Divine Mercy' was set up with the aid of Fr Sopocko in 1941.

The Devotion condemned

In 1958 theologians from the Vatican examined Sr Faustina's diary and then issued a condemnation of it and the Institute. Fr Sopocko was reprimanded and all the work of the Divine Mercy movement was suppressed. The Vatican's action was due to Sr Faustina's poor education; poor spelling, punctuation and unclear sentence constructions which gave rise to fears of heretical teaching. Through the intervention of Karol Wojtyla, then archbishop of Cracow, and the future Pope John Paul II, a fresh investigation was launched. The outcome of this in-depth investigation was that the devotion to the Divine Mercy was once again permitted. Sr Faustina was beatified on 18 April 1993 and canonised by Pope John Paul II on 30 April 2000.

Final approval and affirmation

The Church officially confirmed St Faustina's visions, not only by her canonisation but also by liturgically setting aside one Sunday in the year, the first Sunday after Easter, as Divine Mercy Sunday. Pope John Paul II said on Divine Mercy Sunday, 2001: 'The message that St Faustina delivered to us is the appropriate and incisive answer from God to the questions and fearful expectations of human beings in our time, which is so marked by human tragedies'.

SUMMARY

The approved Liturgy of the Church is the first, and most sure channel of worship and prayer. Over the centuries there have been popular devotions, some promoted by visions and apparitions, which have helped many and enjoyed great popularity. A number of these, notably the Legion of Mary, the Miraculous Medal and the Green Scapular, have faded since the reforms of the Second Vatican Council. These are still available and approved, but they have, in large measure, been succeeded by the popular Divine Mercy devotion and, among others, Celtic spirituality and Creation spirituality.

NOTES – CHAPTER 14

1. The Second Vatican Council's Constitution on the Liturgy, p.143.

CHAPTER 15   *Focus*: CHURCH NOTICE BOARD

OUT INTO THE WORLD

Community of believers

Eager, and perhaps a little apprehensive, on entering the church, our imaginary visitor may have been unaware of the church notice board as he passed through the porch. Departing, a little more at ease, one would hope, the notices for the parish community might catch his attention. Surprisingly, the church notice board is an important symbol. As we have seen, the Catholic Faith does not provide 'spirituality' for lone individuals, it is essentially, since it began on the first Pentecost day (Acts 2:42-47), a community faith; a brother/sisterhood of believers. As Luke describes it, (in Acts 4:32) 'all the believers were one in heart and mind'. All members of a parish have been baptised into the life of the local community, in the name of the family of the Holy Trinity ('I baptise you in the name of the Father and the Son and the Holy Spirit'); and all say together the Christian family prayer, the Our Father. (Preachers have often made much of the fact that there is no 'my' or 'me' in the Lord's Prayer.)

Community news

In the porch our visitor will probably find – if there are any left over from the previous weekend – a copy of the parish newsletter. This is the community's weekly bulletin, sharing, and celebrating, the news of recent baptisms, weddings etc; asking for prayers for sick and housebound members of the parish; reporting on the occasional parish council meetings etc; and advertising future events. These latter could be of a social nature, for building up and developing the social cohesion of the community, like youth events, outings for retired people, singles' club etc; or they may be social events, like a parish dinner or concert, with fund-raising in mind.

Adult formation

Most parish newsletters also provide some simple teaching, or adult formation, in the way of explanation of doctrine, morals or Catholic practice; or it might be just the core of that week's homily from the parish priest. It is widely accepted that the average Catholic's education in their faith finished at primary school level. (Most Catholic parishes have their own primary school.) For this reason every opportunity is taken, in parishes, to provide adult education for those approaching the sacraments, particularly for parents of children to be baptised or making their First Holy Communion.

Notice-board

The posters and notices, on the board in the church porch, supplement the newsletter in providing more details of parish organisations or events; also alerting parishioners to courses and events organised at a Diocesan level. Catholic Aid Agencies, like CAFOD (Catholic Agency for Overseas Development), and perhaps charitable service teams, like those of the SVP (Society of St Vincent de Paul) may have a semi-permanent place on the board.

The Spirituality of CAFOD and SVP

Catholic Agencies that serve the poor and those in any kind of need, not just CAFOD and SVP, but Children's

Societies, Aid to the Church in Need, The Little Way Association and many others, provide Catholics with the opportunity to give expression to their love of God and neighbour. A deep spiritual life, seeking holiness, cannot be attained by the love of God alone; Christ's parable of the Good Samaritan made that quite clear. The Second Vatican Council also makes it clear:

> 'The greatest commandment in the law is to love God with one's whole heart and one's neighbour as oneself (cf. Mt 22:37-40) Christ made this commandment of love of neighbour His own and enriched it with a new meaning. For He wanted to identify Himself with His brothers and sisters as the object of this love when He said, "As long as you did it for one of these, the least of my brothers and sisters, you did it for me" (Mt 25:40). Taking on human nature, He bound the whole human race to Himself as a family through a certain supernatural solidarity and established love as the mark of His disciples, saying, "By this will everyone know that you are my disciples, if you have love for one another" (Jn 13:35)' (para 8).[1]

The above, and what follows, from the same Council document, constitutes the spirituality lying behind the work of CAFOD and SVP and all Catholic Charities.

> 'At the present time, when the means of communication have grown so rapidly, the distances between peoples have been overcome in a sense, and the inhabitants of the whole world have become like members of a single family, works of charity have grown much more urgent and extensive. They can and should reach out to absolutely every person and every need. Wherever there are people in need of food and drink, clothing, housing, medicine,

employment, education; wherever people lack the facilities necessary for living a truly human life, or are tormented by hardships or poor health, or suffer exile or imprisonment, there Christian charity should seek them out and find them, console them with eager care and relieve them with the gift of help. This obligation is imposed above all upon every prosperous person and nation' (para 8).[2]

The Caritas network

As a consequence of these words the Catholic Church, in every corner of the world, set up, through the dioceses, an Aid Agency in every country. Not surprisingly they go by the name *Caritas* (Latin for 'love'). As the Church in England and Wales already had, from 1961, such an agency, it has retained its name of CAFOD; but it works, all the time, with and through its partners, especially the Church's Caritas agency in each country.

Wherever there is need

The words, 'wherever there are people in need' should be noted, because Catholic agencies, like the Caritas network, do not provide aid with any strings attached, nor just to Catholics. The Religion of those in need is of no interest, whether they are Buddhists, Muslims, Hindus, Sikhs or no religion, all equally receive Catholic aid. For example, when I visited Bangladesh (a largely Muslim country) in 2000, with CAFOD, we took £50,000 to relieve the plight of flood victims. The money went to Caritas Bangladesh to provide shelters for the need; most of the money would have been spent on Muslims in need.

Out into the world

The final words of dismissal of the old Latin Mass (replaced by the reforms of the Second Vatican Council) were *Ite missa est*, which, while it literally means 'Go, it is sent', were always translated as 'Go, you are sent out'. The modern English version has captured the meaning with 'Go in peace to love and serve the Lord'. Both have consistently been explained as, 'now that you have expressed your love of God in the Eucharist, go out and express your love for your neighbour in humble service'. In other words, public prayer, on the one hand, and private contemplation on the other, are, in the Catholic tradition, springboards for action; for service to others.

Eucharist and prayer embrace life

Pope Benedict, reports the words of the Bishops at the Synod on the Eucharist, and adds his own comment:

> 'The Christian faithful need a fuller understanding of the relationship between the Eucharist and their daily lives. Eucharistic spirituality is not just participation in Mass and devotion to the Blessed Sacrament. It embraces the whole of life. This observation, the Pope comments, is particularly insightful, given our situation today. It must be acknowledged that one of the most serious effects of the secularisation of our age is that it has relegated the Christian faith to the margins of life as if it were irrelevant to everyday affairs. The futility of this way of living – "as if God did not exist" – is now evident to everyone. Today there is a need to rediscover that Jesus Christ is not just a private conviction or an abstract idea, but a real person, whose becoming part of human history is capable of renewing the life of every man and

woman. Hence the Eucharist, as the source and summit of the Church's life and mission, must be translated into spirituality, into a life lived "according to the Spirit"' (Rom 8:4ff; Gal 5:16, 25).[3]

Contemplation, basis of action

In the same way prayer and contemplation are not personalised ends in themselves, they open us up to be more deeply in love with God, in and through love of our neighbour; and this implies action. As the Cistercian spiritual guide, Thomas Merton comments:

> 'All Christian life is meant to be at the same time profoundly contemplative and rich in active work... When I speak of the contemplative life I do not mean the institutional cloistered life, the organised life of prayer. I am talking about a special dimension of inner discipline and experience, a certain integrity and fullness of personal development, which are not compatible with a purely external, alienated, busy-busy existence. This does not mean that they are incompatible with action, with creative work, with dedicated love. On the contrary, these all go together. A certain depth of disciplined experience is a necessary ground for fruitful action.'[4]

In *No Man is an Island*, Merton expands further:

> 'Action and contemplation now grow together into one life and one unity. They become two aspects of the same thing. Action is charity looking outward to others, and contemplation is charity drawn inward to its own divine source. Action is the stream, and contemplation is the spring.'[5]

Newsletter and notice board challenge

The content, then of the parish newsletter and the notice board is both a witness to the importance of community, and a challenge to put the Christian Faith into action. As the Anglican spiritual writer, Evelyn Underhill, reminds us:

> 'The Church is in the world to save the world. It is a tool of God for that purpose; not a comfortable religious club established in fine historical premises. Every one of its members is required, in one way or another, to co-operate with the Spirit in working for that great end: and much of this will be done in secret and invisible ways. We are transmitters as well as receivers. Our contemplation and our action, our humble self-opening to God, keeping ourselves sensitive to his music and light, and our generous self-opening to our fellow creatures, keeping ourselves sensitive to their needs, ought to form one life; mediating between God and his world, and bringing the saving power of the Eternal into time. We are far from realising all that human spirits can do for one another on spiritual levels if they will pay the price; how truly and really our souls interpenetrate, and how impossible and un-Christian it is to keep ourselves to ourselves.'[6]

One French Catholic, whose efforts to combine contemplation and action, making them 'to form one life' were recognised in 1997, when he was beatified, was Frederic Ozanam. As founder of the SVP (the lay association for personal service of the poor) his influence has been immeasurable for the past 175 years.

Scholar and Catholic Socialist
BLESSED FREDERIC OZANAM (1813-1853)

Frederic was born on 23 April 1813 to Jean Antoine Ozanam, a doctor and Marie Nantas, the heiress to a silk business, at Milan, which was occupied by the French at that time. At 19, Frederic went to Paris to study at the Sorbonne University.

Deeply disturbed by the terrible poverty he witnessed in some parts of Paris in 1833, Frederic, assisted by a group of six fellow Catholic students, set up a society to try and alleviate the extreme conditions. The stimulus for founding what was at first called 'The Conference of Charity', was a heated exchange that Frederic had in a fiery debate on the Church, with a young socialist. The challenge was 'what you say is all theory, what are you doing for the poor, now? Show us your works'. That evening Frederic gathered some friends together, they pooled what little money they had and went out and bought firewood for a couple of poor families.

Through contacts that a Sr Rosalie Rendu had in the neighbourhood, the group started visiting those living in dreadful poverty; distributing clothing, food and linen. The group were reminded of the work and teachings of the legendary St Vincent de Paul. He was a French priest who abandoned the profit to himself of an ecclesiastical career at the Royal Court, in favour of working with the marginalised and forgotten poor of France in the 1600s. (A famous black and white film, called 'Monsieur Vincent', was made and released in 1948; the screenplay was by the acclaimed Jean Anouilh.) The new group decided to adopt St Vincent as their patron and inspiration; so the 'Conference' became the Society of St Vincent de Paul.

In 1839, by the age of 26, Frederic had obtained a Doctorate in Law and Literature and went on to lecture at the Sorbonne, but throughout a glittering academic career he never ceased to support the Society and regularly visit the poor. His weekly experiences of utter poverty directed his thoughts to Catholic socialism and with Lacordaire (an influential Dominican preacher), in 1848, he founded the journal *Ere Nouvelle*, the mouthpiece of their ideas on Catholic socialism. Frederic died, age 40, in 1853, at the height of his illustrious academic career. He was beatified in 1997.

SUMMARY

The church notice board is a symbol of the community dimension of parish life and an avenue and prompt to putting the love of God and love of neighbour into action. CAFOD and SVP (two examples of many Catholic agencies) receive the direction of their spirituality from the Second Vatican Council's decree on the Laity; Christ is personally served, in the serving of whoever is in need. Catholic agencies assist 'whoever' is in need, regardless of their religion, ethnic origins, or social class. Great spiritual writers, like Thomas Merton and Evelyn Underhill, remind us that prayer and contemplation, with action for the needy, form one life, one unity.

BOOK SUMMARY

Catholic Spirituality can be neatly summed up in two words – *Living Faith*. These words can be opened up to refer to – *living the Catholic Faith,* but this would need to be taken with having a daily living faith (in the sense of 'trust in') in the love of God.

Every single one of the many Catholics mentioned in these pages, from the 100 year old lay woman, Catherine Collins, to the great theologian, Cardinal John Henry

Newman, lived by faith. Only faith makes sense of chapters one to fifteen.

NOTES – CHAPTER 15

1. The Second Vatican Council's Decree on the Apostolate of the Laity, p.498.
2. The Second Vatican Council's Decree on the Apostolate of the Laity, p.499.
3. *Sacramentum Caritatis* by Pope Benedict XVI, p.79.
4. *Contemplation in a World of Action* by Thomas Merton, quoted in *Thomas Merton on Prayer*, p.71.
5. *No Man is an Island* by Thomas Merton, quoted in *Thomas Merton on Prayer*, p.27.
6. *The Spiritual Life* by Evelyn Underhill, quoted in *Thomas Merton on Prayer*, p.14.

GLOSSARY

Every walk of life and profession has its own language, not easily accessible to outsiders. The spheres of the Law, the Medical services and Education all have their own vocabulary and jargon; they use a restricted code which has to be learnt if an outsider wishes to meaningfully understand and converse with practitioners. Catholicism is no different. Its theology, moral teaching and whole way of life, depends upon a vocabulary which is not familiar to the ordinary secular person. This glossary is an inadequate attempt to assist the reader who is unfamiliar with the language used in Catholicism. 'Inadequate' because in the very attempt to unravel Catholic terminology, the very same language is occasionally employed.

ALTAR
In ancient times the raised platform or structure on which sacrifices were offered. The word has been applied to the table for the Eucharist since the second century and has been used ever since. According to Canon Law an altar can be 'fixed' in which case it is customary for it to be made of stone; if the altar is 'moveable' it can be of any solid and 'worthy' material. There is an ancient practice of keeping relics of the martyrs under a fixed altar; a link with the Church of the Catacombs.

AMBO
The original name given to the lectern, from which the Scriptures were proclaimed to the people. The raised wooden platform in the early Christian basilicas (some of these have survived the centuries) was replaced by the sixth century by a stone pulpit-like structure; the lectern and pulpit had become one and the same by the fourteenth century. There were no ambos, or even lecterns, in pre-Vatican II churches, the reforms of the Council re-

introduced the structure and the name with the intention of emphasising the dignity and importance of the proclamation of the Word of God.

ANGELUS
A devotional practice, originating in fourteenth-century Europe, that consists in the repetition thrice daily (early morning, noon and evening) of three 'Hail Marys' with versicles (Scripture texts) and prayer, as a memorial of the Incarnation. A bell is rung three times for each 'Hail Mary' and nine times for the closing prayer. The name, *Angelus*, comes from the Latin first word of the opening versicle ('The angel of the Lord appeared unto Mary'). During the Easter season it is replaced by the verse, *Regina coeli laetare, alleluia*. The practice did not come into general use until the seventeenth century.

ARCIC
The Anglican-Roman Catholic International Commission is a joint commission of theologians of the Anglican Communion and the Roman Catholic Church. It started work in 1970 with the intention of seeking 'that unity in truth and faith for which Christ prayed'. The annual meetings of the first Commission produced a series of 'Agreed Statements' on 'Eucharistic Doctrine' (1971); 'Ministry and Ordination' (1973); Authority in the Church (1976). A second Commission was set up in 1982 by Pope John Paul II and Archbishop Runcie; this has produced Agreed Statements on 'Salvation and the Church' (1987); 'The Church as Communion' (1990) and in 2006 'Mary, Grace and Hope in Christ'.

ASH WEDNESDAY
The first day of Lent, six and half weeks before Easter, is called 'Ash' Wednesday because ashes are used that day to symbolise the beginning of the season of penitence. The

practice of having ashes on your head, or your forehead marked with ashes, is very Biblical being mentioned over a dozen times (usually associated with the wearing of 'sackcloth'!). After the reading of the Gospel the priest marks the foreheads of those who come forward (it is an optional practice) with the words, 'Turn away from sin and be faithful to the Gospel' (Mk 1:15).

BAPTISTERY

In the first century Baptisms took place in rivers, lakes and ponds – see the story of Philip baptising the Ethiopian in Acts 8:26-40. Special places were put aside from the middle of the third century (the earliest known baptistery is that at Dura Europos, about 256), at first in the local church and by the seventh century the baptistery was often sited in a separate building. The actual baptismal basin was set in the floor, and cruciform in shape, to emphasise the teaching (found in Romans 6:4) that Baptism was a dying, as Christ died, and a rising up to new life. So the person to be baptised entered on one side, was immersed in the water in the centre and came out the far side; having passed 'through' the cross of Christ to emerge to newness of life, freedom from sin and membership of the community. A white robe would be provided as the new convert stepped out of the water.

BENEDICTINE ORDER

Two monasteries were founded by St Benedict of Nursia, Subiaco and Monte Cassino (central Italy) and he wrote a Rule of Life (c.540), but he did not found an Order. Monasteries in Gaul, England and Germany adopted this Rule and by the ninth century a consciousness had developed among the monks and nuns following this way of life that they all belonged to the family, or Order, of St Benedict. Because each monastery was autonomous and many were very large and wealthy, abuses crept into monastic observance. Cluny (founded 909) was one of the main centres of reform, and by the end of the eleventh century over one thousand monasteries were affiliated to its reforming spirit. Other reform movements followed in the fifteenth century. Evidence of communities of nuns following the Rule of St Benedict goes back to at least the seventh century. A number of illustrious Benedictine nuns, St Hildegard of Bingen, St Gertrude the Great and Mechthild of Magdeburg, illustrate the high degree of spirituality that flourished among them.

BENEDICTION
To this word should be added, 'of the Blessed Sacrament'. A service of exposition of the Blessed Sacrament, which concludes with the people being blessed with the consecrated Host, which is on show, for adoration, in a monstrance. From the sixteenth century this service was comparatively short and in the years prior to the Second Vatican Council it was the principal evening service for Catholics. It began to decline in popularity when evening Masses were permitted.

BIBLE
The word 'Bible' is derived from the Greek for 'books'; however the usual Greek word for the Jewish sacred writings was 'Scripture'. Despite appearances a Bible is not really a book, but a library of books. It is a collection of books accepted by the Church as the inspired, authentic account of God's revelation. It is divided into the Old Testament (another word for 'Covenant') and the New Testament. The Old Testament, written mainly in Hebrew over a period of nearly one thousand years, consists of 46 books: the New Testament is made up of 27 books, written in Greek between 50 AD and 140 AD.

CAFOD
The Catholic Agency for Overseas Development is the official Aid Agency of the Catholic Church in England and Wales. It began back in 1961 when the National Board of Catholic Women organised the first Family Fast Day. Their idea was that Catholic families would be encouraged, in one day in Lent, to cut back on their food for one day and donate the money saved to a Third World (as it was called in those days) project. Not only did the idea catch on – there are two Family Fast Days in the year nowadays – but CAFOD began and was officially adopted by the Bishops of England and Wales. (Scotland and Ireland have their own Aid Agencies.) CAFOD raises funds, principally through Catholic parishes and schools, so that it can promote long-term development, respond to emergencies, raise public awareness of the causes of poverty, speak out on behalf of poor communities, and promote social justice in witness to Christian faith and gospel values.

CANONS
Originating from the Greek word for a straight rod, or measuring stick, in Church life the term came to be used in various ways, one being for 'laws' or regulations; it also came to be used as an ecclesiastical title, particularly for clergy belonging to a cathedral or collegiate church. The Augustinian Canons (also called Austin, Black, or Canons Regular) were priests who, from the eleventh century, tried to live a simple common life, following the Rule of St Augustine of Hippo.

CARTHUSIANS
The Carthusian Order is a strictly contemplative order founded in 1084 by St Bruno at the Grande Chartreuse (whence its name). The monks are vowed to silence and each lives in his own cell within the monastery, working and devoting several hours daily to mental prayer, and

meeting one another, in silence, for the Office, for Mass and for meals on special occasions. During the Reformation a number were put to death by Henry VIII. They have produced many mystics and devotional writers. The headquarters of the English Carthusians is the Charterhouse, Parkminster in West Sussex.

CATHEDRA

This term comes from the Greek for 'a thing sat upon' and it always refers to the official seat or throne of the bishop. Hence the church in which this seat can be found is called a 'cathedral'; the bishop's church where his seat is located. It is undoubtedly the most ancient insignia of a bishop's authority; and many centuries before bishops assumed the wearing of mitres, rings and even the carrying of pastoral staves, called crosiers, the cathedra was the sign of the bishop's role and authority. An excellent and unique example, in England, of a 'cathedra' can be seen in Norwich cathedral, most of which was built in Norman times. (Solemn Catholic definitions on Faith or Morals made by the Pope are only deemed infallible if they are 'ex cathedra'; that is delivered from the seat of the Bishop of Rome.)

CATHOLIC

The word is derived from the Greek for 'universal'. First used in literature by St Ignatius of Antioch (c.100). It has come to have various uses: 1: To refer to the belief that the Christian Church is for all, regardless of culture etc. 2: To distinguish the universal Church from local Christian communities. 3: In historical writers, used of the undivided Church, before the schism of 1054; after which the East referred to themselves as 'Orthodox' and the West as 'Catholic'. 4: Since the Reformation, Roman Catholics have come to use it of themselves exclusively, with Anglicans and Old Catholics associating themselves with the belief that such Communions together represent the undivided

Church of earlier ages. 5: In general, those Christians who claim to be in possession of a historical and continuous tradition of faith and practice; as opposed to Protestants who tend to find their ultimate standards in the principles of the Reformation of the sixteenth century.

CHURCH
Catholics do not worship in a temple, a synagogue, a meeting hall etc. but in a building called 'a church'. The Latin word *ecclesia* comes from the Greek *ekklesia* which means 'an assembly'; primarily it was used of a gathering of citizens, in a self-governing city state. It is clear, from the letters of Paul, that among Greek-speaking Christians, the word *ekklesia* was used from the beginning for both the local community of Christians and for the whole, worldwide, Christian community. So the building, where *the* local 'Church' met, was called *a* church.

CONFESSIONAL
Familiarly nicknamed 'the box' by Catholics who used such, weekly or monthly, in the age before the Second Vatican Council reformed the sacrament of Confession, Penance, or, as it is known these days, Reconciliation. The idea of the confessional was to provide privacy for the penitent who wished to confess to the priest and receive the sacrament of God's forgiveness. (The priest did not – could not – personally forgive the penitent; as in the other sacraments, he was the human 'channel' by which the Risen Christ could absolve the sinner.) Entering 'the box' the penitent would find a kneeler, which faced a covered grill in the wall. On kneeling down, the priest, who was out of sight and could only be heard, would quietly give a blessing. Then the penitent would speak, saying how long it was since he/she were last at the sacrament, then confess whatever serious sins were on their conscience. The priest would impart a few encouraging words and then recite the

absolving prayer of the sacrament. Before the penitent left a small 'penance', usually a number of prayers was given. This would normally be done straightaway when the penitent returned to the body of the church. In these days of concern about abuse, of whatever kind, the confessional, for all its shortcomings, was a secure place where no physical contact was possible.

CONFRATERNITY

The word and concept has the same root as the word 'fraternity' from the Latin *fraternitas* meaning 'brotherhood'. During and after the Middle Ages confraternities were founded in the Church to meet the spiritual and social needs of the clergy and laity. At the beginning the emphasis was upon securing for members mutual support in death through Masses and prayers; however this developed into also providing financial and material assistance. Through their almsgiving they made a considerable contribution to the relief of poverty. By the eighteenth century they had become groups that encouraged personal devotion and pious public acts (e.g. the organisation of and presence in religious processions).

CONGREGATION

In that part of Catholicism called 'The Religious State or Life' there are monks (Religious brothers) and nuns (Religious sisters) who live either the cenobite life, that is a life under a Rule, lived in community with vows; or the eremitical life, which is the life of a hermit, who observes no uniformed way of life. The great and long-founded Religious foundations, like the Benedictines, the Carthusians and Cistercians are 'Orders'. The foundations that have taken place in more modern times, for example, the Passionists in the eighteenth century, are called Congregations.

CORPUS CHRISTI
Officially known, since 1970, as The Feast of the Body and Blood of Christ; although it is still popularly known as 'Corpus Christi' (Body of Christ). The feast commemorates the institution and gift of the Holy Eucharist. The natural day, in the Christian calendar for this would be Maundy Thursday (or Holy Thursday) when the Last Supper is recalled, but the memory of the Passion of Christ on that day in Holy Week made a separate day for the Eucharist desirable. The Thursday after Trinity Sunday was chosen as the first free Thursday after the Easter season.

CRUCIFIX
The figure of the crucified Christ modelled on a cross makes it a crucifix; widely used in the Western Church. In the East, in the Orthodox churches, the flat surface image – an icon – was used instead. In medieval times the rood screen which ran across the centre of the church would be surmounted by a large crucifix. As a central feature, on or above the altar itself, it began to come into use in the thirteenth century. This use has, with adaptation (sometimes the processional cross is used or the cross is surmounted by a figure of the risen Christ) been continued by the Catholic Church. The Council of Nicea in 787 placed icons and the crucifix on the same level of dignity as the Scriptures.

DESERT FATHERS
There were negative effects for the Christian Church, of the Religious tolerance in the Roman Empire (313 AD), following the accession of Constantine. Vast numbers became Christians and the standards dropped; a contemporary writer commented 'there are many more Christians and less Christianity'. Many individual Christians, serious about spirituality, left the corrupt society behind and went to seek a closer union with Christ, having given away their possessions, in a life of solitude in the desert. The most

famous of these hermits (or Desert Fathers and Mothers, as they were called in Christian history) was St Antony (c250-355). They chose their own austerities, which were extreme; some hardly eating or sleeping. The movement, of thousands of such hermits, spread from Egypt to Syria and modern Iraq. Antony encouraged associations and a partial community life, which eventually developed into the monasticism we are now familiar with.

DEVOTIO MODERNA
From the Latin for 'Modern Devotion'. The term is applied to the revival and deepening of Catholic Spirituality from the end of the fourteenth century. This revival of interest and enthusiasm spread from the Netherlands – where it was associated with G. Groote and Thomas à Kempis and his *Imitation of Christ* – to Germany, France and Italy. It laid great emphasis on the inner life of the individual and encouraged methodical meditation, especially on the Life and Passion of Christ. It was spread by secular priests and lay people, who called themselves 'Brethren of the Common Life'.

DOCTOR
A title regularly given, since the Middle Ages, to certain Christian theologians of outstanding merit and acknowledged saintliness. Originally, in the Western (or Latin) Church, Gregory the Great, Ambrose, Augustine and Jerome were held to be the 'four doctors' *par excellence*; but in later times the list has gradually increased to over thirty. The most recent addition being St Thérèse of Lisieux.

ENGLISH MYSTICS
Throughout Europe in the fourteenth and fifteenth centuries there was a great flowering and flourishing of Catholic mystics. In Germany, the Rhineland and Holland, there were great mystics like Meister Eckhart (d.1327),

Henry Suso (d.1366) and Thomas á Kempis (d.1471). England too had its mystics, like Richard Rolle (d.1349), Walter Hilton (d.1396) and Julian of Norwich d.1416). Their writings are still available, and those of Julian of Norwich have been especially popular.

EXPOSITION

To this word should be added, 'of the Blessed Sacrament'. For more than a thousand years of Church history it was not customary to show public devotion to the Reserved, or Blessed, Sacrament. From the eleventh century there were the beginnings of a public manifestation of faith and love of the sacramental presence of Christ. Exposition of the Blessed Sacrament, as a service apart from Mass, is first found in the fourteenth century.

FIRST FRIDAYS

The practice of receiving Holy Communion on the first Friday of nine consecutive months without break (the Nine First Fridays) is based upon a promise that Christ is believed to have made to St Margaret Mary Alocoque (1647-1690). In one of her visions Christ, she reported, promised that everyone who fulfilled this practice would have the grace of full repentance and would not die without receiving the sacraments. Now that most people, who attend Sunday Mass, receive Holy Communion weekly, the practice is rarely observed.

FONT

The word comes from the Latin *fons* meaning 'spring of water' and refers to a receptacle for baptismal water, normally made of stone. In early Christian times, when adult Baptism was the rule, it was a large basin (see Baptistery). It became a smaller basin and higher off the ground when infant Baptism became the norm.

FORTY HOURS' DEVOTION

Also known as *Quarant'Ore or Quarantore*. It is a Catholic devotion which consists in the public adoration of the Blessed Sacrament continually for forty hours. It was first introduced in Milan about 1527. After a special Mass the consecrated host (the Blessed Sacrament) is put on show in a **monstrance** surrounded by candles; worshippers take turns to be present and keep up a stream of adoration and praise (usually in silent prayer) for the period, which closes with another special Mass.

FRANCISCANS

The Order of Friars Minor was founded by St Francis of Assisi in 1209, when he gave his followers a Rule (later lost). A Rule was brought into final form and approved in 1223. The friars were to live by the work of their hands or, if need be, by begging; but forbidden to own property or accept money. The Order has always cultivated popular preaching and missionary activities; it went through turbulent times in the thirteenth and fourteenth centuries mainly centred on how to follow the example of their founder, living in poverty. The Order has produced some great saints, like St Anthony of Padua, and theologians, like St Bonaventure and Duns Scotus. It has promoted popular devotions like the Angelus, the Christmas crib, and the Stations of the Cross.

GOOD FRIDAY

The Friday of Holy Week on which day the Passion and Death of Jesus is recalled and celebrated. Called 'Good' not because it was good for Christ, but because it was good for the human race; Christ's death brought redemption. There are two different times for the service that day (only one is permitted). It is the Catholic tradition to hold the service at the time of Christ's death – 3.00pm. However, the Anglican tradition is to start the service at noon.

HAIL MARY

The best known and most frequently used prayer asking for Mary's intercession. It divides into two; the first half is made up of two quotations from the Bible, being Luke 1:28 and Luke 1:42 joined together. This part dates in the East, from the fifth century but only became common and popular in the West, in the twelfth century. The second part, 'Holy Mary, Mother of God, pray for us sinners now and at the hour of our death' was added in the sixteenth century and received official approval in 1568 when Pope Puis V added it to the Roman Breviary.

HOLY DEATH SPIRITUALITY

During the Middle Ages, and right up to the late nineteenth century, Catholics, due to the over-emphasis upon the sacredness of the consecrated bread and wine of the Eucharist, adored the host, but rarely, in the course of their lives, received Holy Communion. Everyone hoped to receive it on their deathbed, as the viaticum, (from the Latin, 'provision for a journey') along with the anointing of the 'Last Sacraments'. Much of popular spirituality focused upon making a good end and avoiding eternal punishment. Although the practice of receiving Holy Communion improved to at least once a year (and more frequently after the reforms of Pope St Pius X in 1910) the importance of dying a 'holy' death was still paramount in Catholic thinking. The laity expected a priest to be available, on call, in the priests' house at all times, should a parishioner be in a danger of death situation. There were many prayers in popular prayer books for a 'happy and holy death'; and the 'Hail Mary' asks for Mary's intercession 'at the hour of our death'.

HOLY WATER

Water which has been blessed by a priest for certain specific religious purposes. These purposes include, blessings, at funerals, exorcisms, individual personal blessings when entering a church, and the public penitential rite of Asperges at the beginning of Mass. The Christian use of water, other than Baptism, dates from the fourth century in the East and the fifth century in the West.

HOLY WEEK
The last week of Lent culminating with Easter Day, which begins with Palm Sunday (or Passion Sunday) and includes Maundy Thursday and Good Friday.

ICON
The word 'icon' comes from the Greek for 'image' (*eikon*) and was originally applied to a statue, a picture painted or made of mosaic or a drawing scratched on the walls of a catacomb. In more modern times, and associated with the Orthodox Church, the term has become more narrowly applied to representations of Biblical events or saintly figures painted in a definite style and manner. Icon painting (iconography) is governed by strict rules and is viewed as an act of prayer and the resulting icon as a 'gateway' to the Spiritual world and an aid to prayer.

INDULGENCES
The practice of granting or gaining indulgences depends upon the belief that every sin upsets not only God, but the good order of community life, for example, stealing, lying, adultery; so every sin attracts a penalty, to be worked out here or in purgatory. From the third century, in the Church, the penances laid upon sinners could be mitigated by the intercession of the martyrs, those awaiting death for their faith, (this presupposes belief in the Communion of Saints), and later by the prayers and good works of others. Later still, in the eleventh century, the Church allowed alternative good works to replace the penances and the merits of Christ and the saints (that is the 'treasury' of grace won by

Christ and the saints) could be applied, to make up the deficiency. From this teaching the practice of granting indulgences, starting in the twelfth century, became common. (It was open to abuse and some substantial abuses contributed to the Reformation). The whole framework of the teaching was seriously questioned by the Second Vatican Council and substantially revised by Pope Paul VI in January 1967; see his decree *Indulgentiarum doctrina.*

JESUITS
The Society of Jesus was founded by St Ignatius Loyola, with nine companions; it was approved by Pope Paul III in 1540. Its principle aim was through various ministries to work for the propagation of the Faith and to promote the spiritual life among the laity; especially through the 'Spiritual Exercises', which had been written by St Ignatius. The most characteristic institutions of the Society have been the universities (for example, the Gregorian in Rome) and schools founded and staffed by the Society. Peculiar to the Jesuits is a special vow to travel for ministry anywhere in the world that the Pope may order, an indication of the missionary aim that motivated Ignatius and his companions from the beginning. Outstanding among many missionaries was St Francis Xavier in India and Japan, Matteo Ricci in China and Manuel da Nobrega in Brazil.

JULIAN OF NORWICH
English spiritual writer, anchoress and mystic, whose writings have become very popular in modern times. Little is known of her early life, but probably born about 1342. By 1394 she was an anchoress at St Julian's church, Norwich. Her real name is not known; she took her name from the church. In May 1373, during an illness, she received a revelation, consisting of fifteen 'showings'(and one more showing the day after). Her book (the short text)

called *Showings (or Revelations) of Divine Love* was published in 1373. Julian spent the next twenty years meditating on the 'Showings' and published the long text in 1393. She finds in the Passion of Christ the key to understanding all that is wrong with the world. Both 'Texts' are available in print; the Long Text, being the fruit of Julian's meditations is more highly recommended.

LECTERN
From the Latin word 'legere' to read; so the reader is the 'lector', and the book of readings is the 'lectionary' and the stand from which the lector reads from the lectionary is the lectern. This name for the reading stand replaced 'ambo' in the early Middle Ages.

MASS
The popular name for the Eucharist (from the Greek word for 'thanksgiving'). 'Mass' is a late form of the Latin word *missio,* derived from *mittere* 'to send'. Part of the dismissal prayer at the end of the service of the people by the celebrant. (In the Roman Rite *Ite missa est.*) Usage was well established by the early Middle Ages.

MAUNDY THURSDAY
This is the traditional English name for the Thursday of Holy Week, the first day of the three sacred days called the Sacred Triduum. During the evening the memorial meal of the Last Supper and the institution of the Eucharist is commemorated and celebrated.

MONASTERY
The house or establishment of a monastic community of monks or nuns. The modern usage of applying the term to communities of men and calling houses of nuns, 'convents' (or from those ignorant of Catholicism, 'nunneries') has no authority behind it.

MONSTRANCE

The name for this sacred vessel originates from the Latin *'monstro, monstrare'* meaning 'to show', because it is constructed to show off a large consecrated host. When devotion to the Blessed Sacrament began to spread in the later Middle Ages, the Host was first venerated in a closed ciborium or dish, but as time passed a transparent cylindrical container, like a radiant sun, with the host in the centre was used. By the late fifteenth century it had assumed a highly decorated and standard shape. (Many modern Catholics, who are not familiar with **Benediction** have never seen a monstrance.)

NOVENA

A term applied to a period of prayer, of nine days' duration, which can be private or public. It may consist of a simple prayer for nine days, or a more structured public series of services. It is hoped, by the devotion, to obtain some special grace or favour of God. It is a modern practice dating from the seventeenth century, but it is modelled upon the nine days of preparation of the Apostles and the Blessed Virgin Mary for the descent of the Holy Spirit.

PRESBYTERY

In ordinary Catholic parlance this word refers to the Priest's house, usually next door to the church. It originates from the word *presbyter* which, in the earliest days of the Church, referred to the 'elder' (usually in the plural) who had responsibility for the good order of the local Christian community. (See Acts 11:30.)

PRIORY

The religious house presided over by a 'prior' or a 'prioress'. It is the usual name for the residence of mendicant friars (Dominicans, Franciscans etc). Priories were set up by large monasteries in the Middle Ages to supervise properties owned by the monasteries.

RECUSANT
A person who refused to attend the services of the established Church of England, particularly in the sixteenth and seventeenth centuries. From 1570, following the Pope's excommunication of Queen Elizabeth I, it became a very serious problem for Catholics, who were fined heavily, or imprisoned, if they did not attend their local Anglican church on a Sunday. Recusancy was particularly feared by the Elizabethan and Jacobean governments (although they benefited mightily from the tax raised) because the substantial numbers of faithful Catholics in Lancashire, Yorkshire and Durham threatened armed rebellion several times. The weight of taxation, over a long period, eventually crushed the Catholic Church in most of England and Wales. A small recusant Church did survive in some rural parts of Lancashire.

RELICS
In Christian usage the word is used of material remains of a saint after his/her death; as well as sacred objects which have been in contact with a saint's body. There were Scripture antecedents – for example Elijah's mantle and the bones of Elisha – which are based on the natural instinct of people to treat with reverence what is left of the dead they loved. The Christian practice commenced with the remains of the martyrs venerated from an early date. St Jerome (and later St Thomas Aquinas) explained the theology; that the relics of the martyrs were honoured for the sake of Christ, for whom these heroes died.

REREDOS
Any decoration on the east wall of a church above and behind the altar. The earliest forms were paintings of biblical

scenes or symbols; however in the Middle Ages a reredos might consist of rich hangings or a piece of jewelled metal work, as in St Mark's, Venice. More commonly in Northern Europe there would be painted wooden panels or a triptych. Later still the reredos was often of stone, with carved biblical scenes or saints.

RETREAT

A period of days spent in quiet and reflection, apart from the normal run of life; time is spent on meditation and other religious exercises. The Scriptural inspiration for the practice is the forty days spent by Christ in the wilderness and his custom of drawing apart for silent prayer. The Jesuits were the first religious order to include retreats in their rule; and they promoted them for all religious and the clergy. In the seventeenth century retreat houses were instituted, where those who wished to make a retreat might stay for short periods, under the guidance of spiritual directors or 'conductors'. Lay people have become more interested and involved since the Second Vatican Council.

ROSARY

A form of public or private prayer in which, while there is a continuous repetition of 'the Hail Mary' in groups, or decades, of ten, there is a meditation on one of the main events or mysteries of salvation. For example, after reciting the Lord's Prayer, while repeating the Hail Mary ten times the reciter may meditate on the Birth of Jesus, or the presentation of the child Jesus in the Temple. The 'mysteries' are divided into four and are called 'The Joyful', 'The Sorrowful', 'The Luminous' and 'The Glorious'. The public recitation of the Rosary, along with a sermon and Benediction was once a popular Sunday evening service; sometimes repeated during the week.

SACRA TRIDUUM (EASTER TRIDUUM)
The Latin word 'triduum' means a period of three days; so 'sacra triduum' means 'holy three days' and refers to the most sacred and precious days in the Christian calendar; the days celebrating the death and resurrection of Christ. (It needs to be recalled that Catholic practice follows the Jewish practice of starting holy days on the evening before; so for the Jew the Sabbath begins on Friday evening.) The first sacred day starts on Maundy Thursday evening and runs to Good Friday evening. The second day takes us from Good Friday evening to Saturday evening; and the final day (the 'Third Day') runs from Holy Saturday evening to Easter Sunday evening. So the Easter Vigil on Saturday night is already Easter Sunday. No genuine Catholic will miss taking part in the Sacra Triduum.

SACRAMENTS
The word 'sacrament' comes from the Latin *sacramentum* meaning 'that which binds a person' or 'the military oath'. It is used however in early Christian usage to translate the Greek word for 'mystery'. Sacraments are understood, from the beginning to be a sharing in the mystery of the Risen Christ. The fundamental mystery is the Incarnation (the Son of God, second person of the Holy Trinity, becoming a human being) and depending on that, the Church, which St Paul tells us is his body (Col 1:18), through which he communicates himself to humankind. The Catholic Church identifies seven special signs or sacraments of the Risen Christ's action; each uses material things, like water (Baptism), bread and wine (the Eucharist), oil (anointing of the sick), etc, to be 'a visible form of invisible grace' (St Augustine writing in fifth century). The seven sacraments are Baptism, Confirmation, the Eucharist, Reconciliation, Anointing of the Sick, Marriage and the Ordination of Priests.

SANCTUARY

In the earliest churches the altar was placed in a central position so that the people could gather around it, but by the beginning of the fifth century the altar was moved into an area designated for the clergy alone; this was called the *sanctuarium* or sanctuary. A low barrier marked this off from the people in the apse. The area around the altar, including the ambo, is still called the sanctuary.

SCAPULAR

Originally the scapular was part of the habit worn by members of a Religious Order, it was sleeveless and hung from the shoulders to the ground, front and back. When lay people wished to be associated with one of the Orders they were encouraged to wear a simple cloth pendant, only a few inches square and usually worn out of sight under clothing.

SEDILIA

The chair for the celebrant of the Eucharist was replaced in the early Middle Ages with seats for the deacon and sub-deacon who sat beside the celebrant. About the middle of the twelfth century, in English parish churches, these seats became a stone bench, which was moved to the south side of the chancel. The Second Vatican Council restored the celebrant, or presiding minister's chair. No one else, including Extraordinary ministers of the Eucharist, may at any time use this seat.

SEMINARY

The word comes from the Latin for 'seed' *semen*. In Church usage it is a school or college devoted (like a seed-bed) to the nourishing and formation of vocations to the Priesthood. The Council of Trent ordered the establishment of seminaries in every diocese; both junior (minor) for boys from the age of 12/13; and senior (major), in which men were to be formed spiritually, academically and pastorally. The Second Vatican Council's decree on Priestly Formation *Optatam Totius* reformed the seminary system, raising the age at which boys/young men could be accepted for formation.

SIGN OF THE CROSS
One of the distinguishing marks of Catholic Spirituality is the use, in public worship and in private prayer, of the sign of the cross. Tertullian writing about the year 200 AD speaks of it as an 'ancient' practice! He says the 'sign of the Lord' sanctifies every daily action, from rising in the morning to retiring at night. It also appears to have been used as a sign of mutual recognition in times of persecution. In the early centuries the sign was drawn upon the forehead by the thumb. In later times it has been made by drawing the right hand from forehead to breast, and then from shoulder to shoulder.

SPIRITUAL DIRECTOR
One who counsels and directs a person's spiritual life (sometimes called 'a Spiritual Father'). Usually the director is a priest, or male or female religious (some of the best spiritual directors have been nuns). In a religious community, or a confraternity, the Spiritual Father is often designated by those in authority, to guide the novice, member of the community or the student for the priesthood.

STATIONS OF THE CROSS
Also known as 'The Way of the Cross'. A series of fourteen pictures, plaques or carvings, which are designed for devotional use, arranged around the walls of a Catholic church, depicting traditional incidents in the last journey of Christ from Pilate's house to His entombment. They can be privately used at any time, and are publicly used, with meditations and prayers, during Lent. It is believed

that crusaders returning from the Holy Land brought back the practice of pilgrims in Jerusalem, retracing the steps of Christ as he carried his cross to Calvary. Certainly by the late Middle Ages, encouraged by the Franciscans, it was a widespread devotional practice.

STIGMATA
An extremely rare phenomenon, where the wounds of Christ's Passion are reproduced on a person's body. It is usually accompanied by other manifestations of the same category, such as levitation, bi-location and telepathic faculties. The stigmata can be invisible, when the person experiences the pain, but not the visible exterior signs, or visible, when they consist of wounds or blood blisters. The official attitude of the Catholic Church is one of great caution, so guarded that the stigmata is never taken into account when a person is proposed for canonisation. The first recorded case was that of St Francis of Assisi; after him there have been over three hundred cases claimed, of which sixty were saints, like St Catherine of Siena.

STOUP
This is a basin near the entrance of a church containing **holy water** with which the Catholic, entering the church, may bless themselves. They are of various forms, either let into the wall and of stone or free-standing and of any worthy material, for example, copper. They are believed to have originated from the fountain standing in the atrium (first of a Roman house, then the forecourt attached to an early Christian church) in which those who entered washed their hands and faces. From the middle of the ninth century they had become the stone basins seen just outside or in the porches of most pre-reformation English churches. The connection with repentance and Baptism was made about the same time; so that the blessing, in the name of

the Holy Trinity, became a reminder of the believer's commitment.

SVP
The Society of St Vincent de Paul is an international Christian voluntary organisation dedicated to tackling poverty and disadvantage by providing direct practical assistance to anyone in need. Active in England and Wales since 1844, today it continues to address social and material need in all its many forms.

SYNOPTIC GOSPELS
If three of the canonical Gospels, Matthew, Mark and Luke are printed out side by side, and seen together (syn-optic), the amount of subject matter and wording that they share stands out. The many similarities and word order immediately raises questions and a direct literary connection is indisputable. It is commonly accepted by modern scholars that Mark wrote first (probably about 65 AD), and Matthew (c.80) and Luke (c.85) had a copy of Mark in front of them when they, using other material too, wrote their accounts of the Good News.

TABERNACLE
The word is derived from the Latin for tent. In the Old Testament we find that the Hebrews travelling through the wilderness, under Moses leadership, at his direction (Exod 25-31) constructed a 'tent of meeting', which they called the tabernacle. In the Catholic Church, despite con-troversies over the tabernacle's position in the church, in the 1990s, it is of late origin. In general for the first 1,000 years it did not, as we know it, exist! From the very earliest times consecrated bread from the Eucharist was taken, often in a simple woven basket, to the sick who could not attend the community's celebration. With the development, in the Church, of devotion to, and adoration of, the Blessed

Sacrament in the late Middle Ages a safe and dignified place was required for the storing of the consecrated hosts. This receptacle or cupboard could be in the sacristy, or it could be, as in some thirteenth-century churches in a pyx that hung near or over the altar. (A pyx is a small ornamented container, often made of a precious metal.). From the sixteenth century it became gradually more customary to keep the Blessed Sacrament in a receptacle that rose above the altar. Tabernacles standing in the centre of the altar (a practice changed by the Second Vatican Council) did not become common practice until the middle of the nineteenth century. Nowadays the tabernacle should be sited, away from the altar, in a quiet dignified place (often a side chapel) where individuals may pray before the reserved Sacrament.

TRANSUBSTANTIATION
The word coined in the twelfth century, later formulated in the teaching of St Thomas Aquinas, to describe – using the Aristotelian understanding of matter – what theologically happens at the Eucharist. It was considered by the Council of Trent as the 'most apt' term for the conversion (trans-substance) of the whole substance of the bread and wine into the whole substance of the Body and Blood of Christ; leaving the 'accidents' of colour, shape, weight etc untouched. Since 'substance' and 'accidents' are no longer scientifically or philosophically acceptable, the term is rarely used and applies (see ARCIC agreement on Eucharistic doctrine) to the 'mysterious and radical change' rather than to explain how the change takes place.

WALSINGHAM
One of the most important shrines for pilgrimage in the Middle Ages, dedicated to the Virgin Mary. The shrine incorporates a replica of the Holy House of Nazareth said to have been built there in the eleventh century. Destroyed

in 1538, the modern Anglican shrine was restored by the Rev A.H. Patten, starting the work in 1922. The Slipper chapel, about a mile outside the village of Little Walsingham, Norfolk, is the only part of the original Shrine complex to have survived. It was opened in 1934 and is the Catholic pilgrimage centre. The statue of Our Lady of Walsingham at the shrine, and reproduced in churches and schools, is modelled on the imprint found on a pre-Reformation seal; the original not surviving Henry VIII's destruction of the site.

APPENDIX ONE

THE GREAT SPIRITUAL GUIDES AND WRITERS

Catholic Spirituality has been guided and shaped by numerous saints, theologians and writers over many centuries; only the principal deceased ones are listed here.

First Seven Centuries

The elements of what constitutes a 'spiritual life' come progressively to light and maturity in the writings and teachings of the following:

St Clement of Rome (c.96). Bishop of Rome; wrote *Epistle to the Corinthian.*
Hermas (second century). Contemporary of St Clement; composed *The Shepherd.*
Clement of Alexandria (c.150-215). Theologian; *The Instructor.*
St Cyprian (200-258). Bishop of Carthage and martyr; wrote many books.

IN THE WESTERN CHURCH

St Ambrose (333-397). Bishop of Milan; wrote several books.
St Augustine (354-430). Bishop of Hippo and Doctor of the Church. Many works; his famous *Confessions* and *The City of God* are in print.
Cassian (360-435). Considered a saint in the Eastern Church; wrote *Conferences.*
St Leo I, the Great, Pope (440-543). His *Letters* and *Sermons* have been drawn upon and used in the Church's Liturgy.

St Benedict of Nursia (480-543). The 'Patriarch of Western monastercism'; his *Rule* for monastic life has been seminal for most monks in the West.

St Gregory I, the Great (540-604). Pope and Doctor of the Church; many books but particularly *Liber Regulae Pastoralis*.

IN THE EASTERN CHURCH

St Athanasius (297-373). Bishop of Alexandria; his *De Incarnatione* is his most famous work, but his *Life of St Antony* was most influential.

St Cyril (315-386). Bishop of Jerusalem; his most influential work is *Catechetical Lectures*.

St Basil, the Great (330-379). One of the great 'Fathers' of the Eastern Church; his *On the Holy Spirit* was his greatest work.

St John Chrysostom (347-407). Bishop of Constantinople and Doctor of the Church; vast volume of writings, his *Homilies* being the most important.

St Cyril (d.444). Patriarch of Alexandria; his most important book is *Book of Treasures on the Holy and Consubstantial Trinity*.

Dionysius the Pseudo-Areopagite (c.500). 'Pen name' of probably Hypatius, Bishop of Ephesus; his *Mystical Theology* and *The Divine Names* are his greatest works.

St John Climacus (c.570-c.649). Abbot of Sinai and ascetical writer, whose *Ladder of Paradise* was very influential in the Middle Ages.

St Maximus the Confessor (c.580-662). Theologian and prolific spiritual writer; one of his noted works was *Treatise on Asceticism*.

There were no writers of importance in the eighth and ninth centuries.

The Middle Ages

1. THE BENEDICTINE TRADITION

St Anselm (1033-1109). Archbishop of Canterbury, foremost of medieval philosophers and theologians; of many writings his *Meditations and Prayers* and *Cur Deus Homo* stand out.

St Bernard (1090-1153). Abbot of Clairvaux; his prolific writings deeply influenced the Middle Ages; his best known work was *Sermons on the Song of Songs*.

St Hildegarde (1098-1179). Abbess; wrote of her visions in *Scivias*.

St Mechthild of Magdeburg (c.1207-1282). Author of a book of mystical Revelations, *Love of the Sacred Heart*.

St Bridget of Sweden (c.1303-1373). Founder of the Bridgettine Order; her *Book of Revelations* was highly esteemed in late Middle Ages.

2. THE AUGUSTINIAN TRADITION

Hugh of St Victor (1097-1141). Prolific writer on all subjects; his *De Sacramentis Christianae Fidei* was very influential in twelfth century Europe.

Adam of St Victor (twelfth century). The most important liturgical poet of the Middle Ages.

3. THE CARTHUSIAN TRADITION

Guigo II (d.1188). Ninth prior of the Grand Chartreuse; one of the most influential spiritual writers of the Middle Ages, remembered particularly for his *Scala Claustralium;* and his guide to *Lectio Divina*.

Ludolf of Saxony (d.1378). Influential writer, best remembered for his *Commentary on the Psalms* and his *Life of Christ*.

Dionysius the Carthusian (1402-1471). Given the title 'Ecstatic Doctor' by his contemporaries; prolific writer of 187 spiritual books.

4. THE DOMINICAN TRADITION

St Dominic (1170-1221). Founder of the Order of Preachers (DominicanOrder); the intensity of his single-minded determination was a powerful spiritual force.

St Albert the Great (d.1280). One of the greatest of Medieval theologians; wrote many books on the Spiritual life.

St Thomas Aquinas (1225-1274). Known as 'the Angelic Doctor'; greatest theologian of the Middle Ages, author of countless works (*Summa Theologiae* being the most famous), including many on Spirituality.

St Vincent Ferrer (1346-1419). Theologian, whose *De Vita Spirituali* was considered a masterpiece.

St Catherine of Siena (1347-1380). Dominican tertiary. Powerful and influential spiritual figure in her time; many writings.

5. FRANCISCAN TRADITION

St Francis of Assisi (1181- 1226). Founder of the Franciscan Order. Besides his amazing personal witness; *The Rule* and *The Canticle of the Sun* (1225).

St Bonaventure (1221-1274). Theologian, known as 'Doctor Seraphicus'; very influential writings, principally *The Soul's Progress to God*.

Ramon Llull *(also Lull)* (c.1233-1315). Franciscan preacher and visionary who worked among the Jews and Muslims; *The Art of Contemplation* was very influential; he is considered a fore-runner of St John of the Cross.

Bl. Angela of Foligno (c.1248-1309). Mystic and Franciscan tertiary; her visions recorded in '*Liber Visionum et Instructionum*'.

6. INDEPENDENT WRITERS

Nicholas of Cusa (1401-1464). German Cardinal, philosopher and reform Preacher; his best known spiritual work is *The Vision of God*.

St John Eudes (1601-1680). French priest who founded two congregations of Religious, he shares with St Margaret Mary Alacoque the claim to have initiated devotion to the Sacred Heart of Jesus. His major work was *The Life and Kingdom of Jesus in Christian Souls*.

Angelus Silesius (1624-1677). *(Johannes Scheffler)*. A convert to Catholicism and priest, wrote mystical poetry; *The Cherubic Wanderer*.

St Vincent de Paul (1581-1660). Founder of Lazarist Fathers and the Sisters of Charity; copious correspondence and spiritual notes.

Jean-Jacques Olier (1608-1657). French priest and founder of the Society and seminary of Saint-Sulpice (a community of secular priests). His spirituality owed much to St Vincent de Paul.

Jacques-Benigne Bossuet (1627-1704). French bishop of Meaux and famous preacher; many writings including *Meditations on the Gospel*.

St John Baptist de La Salle (1651-1719). A priest of Saint-Sulpice he founded the Brothers of the Christian Schools (Christian Brothers).

St Louis Grignion de Montfort (1673-1716). French priest who promoted devotion to the Blessed Virgin Mary; his *True Devotion to the Blessed Virgin Mary* was very influential.

St Alphonsus Liguori (1691-1787). Founder of Redemptorists, moral theologian and successful preacher; a most prolific devotional and spiritual writer; his *Complete Ascetical Works* contains his serious writings.

7. THE GERMAN MYSTICS

Meister Eckhart (d.1327). A Dominican influential spiritual writer whose later work was condemned by the Church. Founder of the German School of Mystics.

John Tauler (d.1361). Dominican spiritual writer and guide;

had lasting influence on later German piety, both Catholic and Protestant.

Blessed Henry Suso (c.1295-1366). *pen name 'Amandus'*. German Dominican spiritual writer, like Tauler influenced by Eckhart; best known book *The Little Book of Eternal Wisdom*.

Blessed John Ruysbroeck (or Jan van Ruusbroec). (1293-1381). One of the greatest of European mystics (given title *Doctor Extaticus*).

A member of a Canons Regular community that was foundational in promoting **Devotio Moderna**. Prolific writer, twelve of his books have come down to us.

8. THE FLEMISH SPIRITUAL WRITERS

Gerard Groot (Geert de Groote). (1340-1384). Founder of the Brethren of the Common Life . Lay missionary preacher and teacher.

Thomas a Kempis (c.1380-1471). First belonging to the Brethren of the Common Life, then Canons Regular; almost certainly the author of the popular and influential *Imitation of Christ*.

9. THE ENGLISH MYSTICS

Richard Rolle (d.1349). Yorkshire man, hermit and spiritual writer. Many popular and influential books, including *The Fire of Divine Love*.

Walter Hilton (d.1396). Nottingham Augustianian Canon; famous for his *The Scale of Perfection*.

Author of *Cloud of Unknowing* (contemporary of Hilton). Anonymous spiritual writer, whose principal work was hailed the greatest mystical writing of fourteenth century.

Julian of Norwich (1342-1416?). Anchorite and spiritual writer of Norwich, Suffolk. Her book *Showings* or *Revelations of Divine Love* available in short or long (preferable) versions. Ever popular.

Sixteenth century to Modern times

1. THE IGNATIAN TRADITION

St Ignatius (1491-1556). Founder of the Jesuits. His great and influential work is the *Spiritual Exercises* which encapsulates many of the spiritual insights and experiences of preceding centuries.

St Robert Bellarmine (1542-1621). Jesuit priest, scholar and controversialist; principal work *The Mind's Ascent to God.*

St Claude de Colombiere (1641-1682). Jesuit priest; best known book *Sufferings of Our Lord Jesus Christ.*

Jean Pierre de Caussade (1675-1751). Jesuit and ascetical writer; who did much to rehabilitate mysticism after Quietism, especially with his famous *Abandonment to Divine Providence.*

Jean-Nicolas Grou (1731-1803). French Jesuit priest, teacher and spiritual writer, best remembered for *Meditations on the Love of God.*

2. CARMELITE TRADITION

St Teresa of Avila *(St Teresa of Jesus).* (1515-1582). Spanish Carmelite nun, mystic and energetic reformer. Her epoch-making influence as a spiritual writer is incalculable. Many writings, especially *The Way of Perfection, The Interior Castle* and her *Life.*

St John of the Cross (1543-1591). Carmelite priest and Doctor *(to be distinguished from the Dominican St John of the Cross* (1505-1560). Disciple of, and co-worker with, St Teresa in founding the Discalced Carmelites. His magnificent four works make up a complete treatise on mysticism. *The Ascent of Mount Carmel, The Dark Night of the Soul, The Living Flame* and *The Spiritual Canticle.*

Brother Lawrence *(Nicholas Herman).* (1611-1691). French Carmelite lay brother, honoured and revered widely for his simple, short *Practice of the Presence of God.*

3. THE TRADITION FROM ST FRANCIS DE SALES

St Francis de Sales (1567-1622). Bishop of Geneva, one of the leaders of the Counter-Reformation; tried to make Spirituality simple for ordinary folk. Many books, particularly *Introduction to the Devout Life* and *The Love of God* which have influenced millions.

St Jane Frances de Chantal (1472-1641). Foundress of the Order of the Visitation; many of her published papers were influential.

St Margaret Mary Alacoque (1647-1693). Chief founder of devotion to the Sacred Heart of Jesus prompted by a series of visions. (Officially recognised 75 years after her death.)

4. MODERN TIMES – INDEPENDENT WRITERS

John Henry Newman (1801-1892). Cardinal *(cause for canonisation going through)*. Drew his inspiration from the Fathers of the Church; his *Meditations and Devotions* and *Sermons* were popular in his day.

Frederick William Faber (1814-1864). Oratorian and hymn writer. Wrote many devotional hymns, devotional books and spiritual guides, including *Growth in Holiness*.

Gerard Manley Hopkins (1844-1889). English convert to Catholicism, Jesuit priest and a major inspirational poet. Output small, but spiritually rich and deep.

Bl Columba Marmion (1858-1923). Irish Benedictine abbot of Maredsous; gifted spiritual writer and director. Main works: *Christ Life of the Soul* (sold 100,000 copies in 1919 alone!) and *Christ in His Mysteries*.

Charles de Foucauld (1858-1916). French explorer and 'Hermit of the Sahara'; the witness of his life, his letters and his Rule for Little Brothers and Sisters of Jesus.

Francis Thompson (1859-1907). English poet, who spent many years living on the streets of London, before rescuing by Wilfred Meynell; his best known poem is *The Hound of Heaven*.

Alban Goodier (1869-1939). Jesuit Archbishop of Bombay; popular spiritual writer, best known work *The Inner Life of the Catholic*.

St Thérèse of Lisieux (*St Teresa of the Child Jesus*). (1873-1897). French Carmelite nun; her autobiographical *Story of a Soul* (with its Little Way) was an international world bestseller. Declared a Doctor of the Church in October 1997.

Teilhard de Chardin (1881-1955). French Jesuit, mystic and famous Scientist, field of paleontology; best known work *Le Milieu Divin*.

Frank Duff (1889-1980). Layman, one of the first ever to speak at a Council of the Church; founder of the Legion of Mary, responsible for the spiritual development of millions of Catholics worldwide.

Fulton J. Sheen (1895-1979). Archbishop, writer and popular broadcaster, his weekly programme *Life is Worth Living* inspired millions; his *To Know Christ Jesus* was a best seller.

Karl Rahner (1904-1984). Jesuit priest and one of the most eminent theologians of twentieth century; his theology influenced the Second Vatican Council. Many theological and spiritual writings including *Prayers for a Lifetime* and *Faith in a Wintry Season*.

Leon-Joseph Suenans (1904-1996). Belgian cardinal, archbishop of Malines, a major influence on Second Vatican Council, credited with the *Gaudium et Spes* document. Very influential in guiding the Charismatic movement through turbulent times. Books include: *The Gospel to Every Creature* and *A New Pentecost?*

Rene Voillaume (1905-2003). French priest who founded the Little Brothers of Jesus, based on the Rule of Charles de Foucauld. Many writings, most important being *Seeds of the Desert*.

Dietrich Bonhoeffer (1906-1945). German Lutheran pastor and founder member of the Confessing Church, that resisted Hitler. His writings and inspiring example (one of twentieth-century martyrs in stone over the Great West door of Westminster Abbey) reached far beyond his own denomination. Books include: *The Cost of Discipleship, Letters and Papers from Prison.*

Bede Griffths (1906-1994). Benedictine monk and sannyasi; dedicated his life to exploring Eastern, especially Indian, forms of prayer and meditation. Established the Saccidananda Asharam and wrote many books on vision of Christ hidden in the world's religions.

Simone Weil (1909-1943). French Jewish writer; deeply drawn to Catholicism, but never converted. Her best known work is *Waiting on God.*

Carlo Carretto (1910-1988). Lay activist and Little Brother of Jesus who spread the fame of Charles de Foucauld; of his dozen spiritual books *Letters from the Desert* was the most influential. Many writings, most important being *Seeds of the Desert.*

Bl. Mother Teresa of Calcutta (1910-1997). Foundress of Missionaries of Charity; most powerful public example of the Spiritual life in late twentieth century; few writings, however *Something Beautiful for God,* book and TV programme, was sensationally successful.

Anthony Bloom (1914-2003). Orthodox Metropolitan archbishop of Western Europe; his talks and books on prayer were extremely popular in 1960s and '70s. Books include: *School of Prayer* and *We Believe in God.*

Thomas Merton (1915-1968). Trappist monk of Gethsemane Abbey, Kentucy; probably the most influential and powerful spiritual writer of the twentieth century. He popularised traditional Western spirituality in many books, articles, etc. His books include autobiographical *Elected Silence* (English version) and *Contemplative Prayer.*

Roger Schutz (1915-2005). Better known as *Brother Roger of Taize.* Founder of the ecumenical religious community of brothers at Taize (Burgundy, France). Inspirational spiritual guide who attracted thousands (especially young people) to Taize; his regular 'letters' and the music from the community influenced hundreds of thousands world-wide. Books include: *Struggle and Contemplation*.

Oscar Romero (1917-1980). Inspirational archbishop of San Salvador, popularly known as *Monsenor Romero*. Champion of the preferential option for the poor; his weekly spiritual broadcasts uplifted and gave hope to an oppressed people. He witnessed to his teaching with his murder. He is one of the ten twentieth-century martyrs, in stone, above the Great West door of Westminister Abbey, London.

Michel Quoist (1921-1997). French priest and industrial chaplain, who worked among poor, and with young people, especially in Le Havre although he had a glittering academic background. His best selling *Prayers of Life*, (1963), translated into 27 languages, revolutionised, across all Christian boundaries, thousands of people's approach to prayer. His other famous books, *Christian Response* and *Christ is Alive* were also influential.

John Main OSB (1926-1982). A Benedictine monk who introduced new ways of meditating; launched many meditations groups in London, Montreal, Canada; grew to become the ecumenical *World Community for Meditation*. Author of several seminal books.

Anthony de Melo (1931-1987). Jesuit priest, psychotherapist and Spiritual guide. His many Spiritual books are widely admired.

Henri Nouwen (1932-1996). Dutch priest, pastor and spiritual guide. Prolific writer, best remembered for *Return of the Prodigal Son*.

Spiritual writers in the Orthodox and Reformed Traditions influenced some Catholic writers, but space here does not permit of their listing.

APPENDIX TWO

SOME FALSE SPIRITUAL PATHS

Docetism as found in the Early Church was a tendency, rather than a formulated doctrine, which considered the humanity and sufferings of the historical Christ to be apparent rather than real. In other words, Jesus Christ was divine and the Son of God, but not actually human; he did not really suffer pain or experience daily life in the same way that we do. The Church condemned this teaching in the early Church Councils. Docetism destroys the meaning of the Incarnation and renders the Redemption by Christ to be impossible, because he could not be a genuine mediator if he were not completely human. Ancient as this teaching is, there are still Catholics in our churches who do not really appreciate how totally human Christ was, like us in all things, but sin (2 Cor 5:21).

Jansenism takes its name from Cornelius Jansen (1585-1638) author of *Augustinus,* which taught that everything is determined. The movement spread a rigorist teaching about morals and was deeply pessimistic, stressing the unworthiness and sinfulness of the human condition. People were crushed by the difficulty of achieving salvation; reception of the Eucharist was discouraged. The movement was declared heretical in 1653, but many years passed before it was finally repressed.

New Age Movement is impossible to define, by its very nature. Unlike most formal religious traditions, it has no sacred text, no central organisation, no clergy, no geographical centre, no doctrine or creed etc. Even in the Movement they often use mutually exclusive definitions for some of their terms. New Age is a free-flowing Spiritual movement, a network of believers and practitioners who share somewhat similar beliefs and practices, which they may add on to whatever established traditional religion that they follow.

Quoting John Naisbitt:

> In turbulent times, in times of great change, people head for the two extremes; fundamentalism and personal spiritual experience... With no membership lists or even a coherent philosophy or dogma, it is difficult to define or measure the unorganised New Age movement. But in every major U.S. and European city, thousands who seek insight and personal growth cluster around a metaphysical bookstore, a spiritual leader or an education centre. *Megatrends 200*, J. Naisbitt.

Some New Age Thought:

> All is God and God is all. God is the real self of everyone. Ignorance is sin. Knowledge brings enlightenment of who you are, so get enlightened – know the Self and know that you are God. I am God, you are God and everything is God. The trees are God, the earth is God, stones are God and the animals are God. Everything must be treated with respect because it is God. *Maze of Deception*, B. Risdon.

Pietism originated in late seventeenth-century Germany Protestantism, where it was rampant. It influenced Catholicism in the France of the eighteenth century, with the Enlightenment and Reason crowned as the answer to everything. Also dominating secular thought and attacking the Church was agnostic Liberalism. Faced with these onslaughts the Church, lacking in a credible response, retreated from science, philosophy and politics and concentrated all its attention on piety and devotional practices. The Church was turned in on itself, narrow and isolationist. Individual Christians can seek a pious independence and individualism, not wishing to be part of the Christian community. However, belonging and sharing in the life of the community has been an essential element of Christianity since the first Pentecost Day.

Quietism, this is a term which is used rather loosely of any system or method of spirituality that minimises human activity and responsibility. It is more usually applied to the teaching of some seventeenth-century spiritual writers, particularly Miguel de Molinos and to a lesser degree Madam Guyon and Archbishop Fenelon. The basic idea behind Quietism is an exaggerated version of abandonment to God. St Teresa of Avila had taught abandonment, but not to the degree of complete passivity and annihilation of will; so passive as to not even care about one's own salvation. One of the results of Quietism was to bring contemplation into disrepute. Molinos' teaching was condemned by Rome, in 1687.

Syncretism was existing at the time of Christ, when in the Mediterranean civilisation attempts were made to combine aspects of the Greek and Roman religions. It was used in the seventeenth century by G. Calixtus, who tried to combine the teaching of the German Reformed Churches with Catholicism. In the twentieth and twenty-first centuries it is the 'pick and mix' approach of some to religion; selecting beliefs from different World Faiths that they like and disregarding those that do not appeal, to concoct their own set of beliefs.

APPENDIX THREE

APPARITIONS OF THE BLESSED VIRGIN MARY

A non-exhaustive listing

While many Catholics experience great spiritual benefits from going on pilgrimage, for example, to Lourdes, it remains true that most Catholics have never been there, or to any of the Marian shrines. Many feel no need, or interest, to do so, while large numbers of those who make such a pilgrimage, find it so spiritually rewarding that they return again and again. Of the six million pilgrims who visit Lourdes each year, very many have repeatedly visited the Shrine.

The first alleged apparition of Mary, the Mother of God, is reported to have been to St Gregory Thaumaturgus, who died in 270 AD. His biographer, St Gregory of Nyssa (d.394) reports that at the time when Gregory became a bishop, he was distressed when he studied the heresies that were current at the time. His earnest prayers for help were answered by an apparition of Mary, accompanied by St John. Mary asked the Evangelist to assist the new bishop; this support, Bishop Gregory believed, gave him the confidence that he needed to counter the heresies.

Another example, from this early period, was recorded in sixth-century art, in the church of the Guides, in Constantinople. A legend tells how the Virgin Mary appeared to two blind men. She took them back to that church, where she restored their sight.

There were quite a number of legendary stories of apparitions circulating in the Middle Ages. Listed below are alleged apparitions that have been carefully recorded and enjoy some kind of ecclesiastical approval.

Date	Person	Place	Detail
2 Aug 1218	Pierre Nolasque	Paris	BVM* asks for a new religious order that will win release of slaves and captives.
15 Aug 1233	Pierre de Todi		Mary gave details of a new Religious Order 'The Servants of Mary'.
Lent 1407	Dominique Helion		He gave his last coins to a beggar woman in 'a blue coat'. When certain promises were fulfilled, Dominique realised it had been BVM.*
3 May 1491	Thierry Schoere	Neidermorschwhir, Alsace	BVM appeared holding some ice and three ears of corn, (Our Lady of the Three ears of Corn).

*Blessed Virgin Mary

ate	Person	Place	Detail
1515	Anglese de Sagazan	Garaison (nr Tarbes)	Mary appeared three times near the source of the river Cier. She asked for a chapel to be built; it was in 1540.
1519	Jean de la Baume	Cotignac, France	
9 Dec 1531	Juan Diego	Hill of Tepeyac, Guadalupe, Mexico	BVM asked for a sanctuary to be built; local bishop convinced with a gathering of roses (Our Lady of Guadalupe).
1579	Matryona	Kazan, Russia	Several apparitions revealed the whereabouts of the icon of Our Lady of Kazan.
1641	Hendrick Busman & Mechel Schrouse	Kevelar, Germany	'Our Lady of Graces'.
May 1664	Benoite Rencurel	Le Laus, France	'Our Lady of Laus'; asks for pilgrimages to the shrine.

Date	Person	Place	Detail
18-19 July & 27 Nov 1830	Catherine Laboure	Rue du Bac, Paris	Mary asks for a medal to be struck – known as the Miraculous Medal.
25 Mar 1831	Seraphim of Sarov (of the Russian Orthdox Church)	not recorded	BVM accompanied by St John the Baptist and St John the Evangelist.
28 Jan 1840	Justine Bisqueyburu	Paris	Justine was given the design of a new scapular, the Green Scapular, to be worn.
20 Jan 1842	Alphonsus Ratisbonne	Rome	Alphonsus was an unbeliever, but the apparition brought his conversion.
19 Sept 1846	Melanie Calvat & Maximin Girard	La Salette, French Alps	'Our Lady of La Salette', reconciler of sinners.

Date	Person	Place	Detail
Feb–Apr 1858 (18 apparitions)	Bernadette Soubirous	Lourdes, France	'I am the Immaculate Conception' BVM asks for people to pray, do penance: also build a church and go on pilgrimage.
1861	Richetto Cionchi	San Luca, Italy	
17 Jan 1871	Eugene Barbelette, Joseph Barbelette, Francoise Richer, Jeanne-Marie Lebosse & Auguste Avice	Pontmain, France	'Our Lady of Hope', children admonished to pray.
15 Feb 1876	Estelle Faguette	Pellevoisin, near Tours, France	Estelle cured and 12 appearances: of 'Mother of Mercy'.
1877	Justina Szafrynska, & Barbara Samulowska	Gietrzwald, Poland	BVM, 'Queen of the Rosary'.

Date	Person	Place	Detail
21 Aug 1879	Mary Byrne & fifteen witnesses	Knock, Ireland	BVM appears with St Joseph and St John the Evangelist.
13 May–13 Oct 1917	Lucia dos Santos, Jacinta Marto, Francisco Marto	Fatima, Portugal	Apparitions on the 13th of each month. 'I am the Lady of the Rosary: 70,000 people see the miracle of the sun.
29 Nov–3 Jan 1932–1933	Fernande, Gilberte & Albert Voisin; Andre & Gilberte Degeimbre	Beauraing, Belgium	33 apparitions, most in silence: 'I am the Immaculate Virgin'.
15 Jan to 2 Mar 1932	Mariette Beco	Banneux, Belgium	BVM makes herself known as the 'Virgin of the Poor'.
8–14 Dec 1947	Nicole Robin, Jacqueline & Jeannette Aubry, Laura Croizon	L'Ile Bouchard, France	Ten encounters between the children and 'Our Lady of Prayer'

Date	Person	Place	Detail
2 April 1968-9	General public, incl. TV (mainly members of Orthodox Church) investigated and approved by Coptic Patriarch, 4 May 1968	Zeitoun, Egypt	Seen by millions of people in person and on television. Photos on internet: enter – 'Appearance of BVM at Zeitoun, Cairo'.
24 June 1981 to present	Originally six young Croatian Catholics; now two.	Medugorje Bosnia-Herzegovina	Still under investigation; public pilgrimages not approved.
1981-1983	Alfonsine Mumureke, Anathalie Mukamazimpaka, Marie-Claire Mukangango, Stephanie Mucamurenzi, Vestine Salima, Emmanuel, Segatashya & Agnes Kamagaju.	Kibehao, Rwanda	Officially recognised in June 2001 'Mary, Mother of the Word'.

The *Lourdes Magazine,* (issue 150, Summer 2007) the official journal published by the Pilgrimage Bureau supplied some of the information for this Appendix. In that issue of the magazine, Jean Longere, president of the French Society of Marian Studies writes of his research.

'Our investigations covered some twenty apparitions, all recognised to varying degrees. This number must be considered in relation to others. In *Cahiers Marials* of 1 April 1971, Dom Bernard Billet had published a list of one hundred and five unrecognised apparitions since 1928. After being sent further information by friends, the number was increased to two hundred and ten, then two hundred and thirty-two from 1920 to around 1975. There are some peaks, for example, in 1933 there were fourteen apparitions, in 1947-1948, there were thirty-nine claims and in 1954, eighteen alleged apparitions.

For his part, Yves Chiron recorded 362 apparitions in twentieth century until 1993. He noted the very rare approved cases, the majority being left 'pending' or with a 'negative decision' on the part of Church authorities. Yves Chiron concludes 'the number of apparitions attributed to Mary, but not recognised, is immediately striking because it is widespread and continuous.'

The content of the messages from the Blessed Virgin Mary through all these alleged apparitions is constant and continual. It is in line with the Gospel message of Scripture, viz. the call to repentance and the repeated call to prayer.

No matter how important the penitential message of Mary seems to be, it seems to come later and is less universal than that of prayer. Prayer really forms the core of the apparitions: that of Mary with the seers, and the prayer she recommends to the Christian people through them. Personal prayer, pilgrimage prayer, prayer in the chapels that Mary so often asks for, or those the Christian people spontaneously build.

Steps to obtain official Church acknowledgement, and recognition of a claim of an apparition are slow and painstakingly ponderous. After the involvement of the local parish priest (who in the case of Bernadette of Lourdes, was very dismissive, until he heard her use theological terminology that she could never have known naturally) the matter is referred to the diocesan bishop. If he believes that there is sufficient evidence, the bishop will appoint an investigative team, who will thoroughly examine the evidence and interview witnesses, etc. If this reports back favourably to the bishop, the matter will be referred to the National Conference of Bishops of that country, who will set up a separate, independent, commission of their own to investigate the claims. Most alleged apparitions and other phenomena, like weeping statues, do not get this far. (By now the appropriate authorities in Rome will have been informed, who will caution that great care is taken.) People will already be visiting the place of the alleged occurrence and the first authoritative decree authorises pilgrimages and public worship at the place. The second decree, some time later recognises the supernatural aspect of the events, which were the origin of a pilgrimage or devotion. A recent example of this is the apparitions of Kibehao in Rwanda (from 1981-1983) which were recognised in June 2001; the first decree authorising pilgrimages had been issued in 1988.

CASE STUDY:

Rome finds flaws in vision claims

A news item in *The Tablet* of 29 October 2007, reported that the Vatican had rejected the claims of Patricia de Menezes, a 67-year-old Catholic woman of Surbiton, Surrey, England, that she was having visions and receiving messages from the Virgin Mary. Mrs de Menezes had founded the Community of Divine Innocence and submitted its statutes to the Vatican for approval. Archbishop Angelo Amato, secretary of the Congregation for the Doctrine of the Faith, conducted an investigation into the community and Mrs de Menezes' claims. Subsequently he wrote to the local bishop, Archbishop Kevin McDonald, expressing grave concerns about the 'exaggerated claims' and the' bizarre' and 'hysterical' words, and the problematic doctrine contained in the visionary's messages. In a statement Archbishop McDonald said that in the light of these concerns about the visions, and the Community of Divine Innocence, no recognition was accorded by the Vatican or the Archdiocese of Southwark. The Community responded by saying that it would continue to propagate its message.

APPENDIX FOUR

CATHOLIC SPIRITUALITY: THE IMPACT OF THE SECOND VATICAN COUNCIL

The Council opened up the Liturgy to ensure that 'the people take part knowingly, actively, and fruitfully'.

Before Vatican II	After Vatican II
Liturgy in Latin – missals required many prayed their rosary.	Liturgy in Vernacular – missals not required, private devotional practices discouraged.

The complex liturgies of High Mass, Sung Mass and Low Mass were replaced 'by a noble simplicity'. 'Rites should be short, clear, and unencumbered by useless repetitions; they should be within the people's powers of comprehension.'

Liturgical music – Gregorian chant and 'Victorian' hymns.	Popular (folk) music – then new compositions, based upon Scripture.
At Mass altar servers responded for the people.	People respond for themselves.
Fasting from midnight meant people only received Holy Communion at early morning Mass.	All encouraged to share at every Eucharist.
People received hosts on the tongue – never from the chalice.	People may receive in the hand and under both kinds.
Priest read all the Scripture texts from the altar, first in Latin; then repeated in English from the pulpit.	Lay readers proclaim first two texts from the ambo.

Before Vatican II	After Vatican II
Women forbidden to enter the sanctuary during the Mass.	Women encouraged to be readers and distribute Holy Communion as Extraordinary Ministers.
Masses only on Sunday mornings.	Evening Masses and Vigil Masses (Saturday evenings) permitted.
Same two Scripture readings on a Sunday, each year.	Three-year cycle of three Scripture readings; 'to open up more lavishly the treasures of the Bible' (Vatican II 'Sacred Liturgy').
Often no sermon/homily at Sunday Mass.	Homily on Scripture mandatory on Sunday.
Sunday evening service of Rosary, Sermon and Benediction.	Evening Mass.
Individual secret confession to priest in confessional.	Reconciliation services: penitent uses private or face-to-face in special room.
Holy Week and Easter services in Latin and 'obscure'; little emphasis on Easter mysteries.	The Paschal Mystery (the significance of Easter) becomes central to the life of the Church.

The Liturgical changes made a big impact upon the spiritual lives of Catholics; just two examples – their lives were enriched by a wider and deeper access to Scripture, with weekly commentary; the dignity of women was enhanced and active participation bestowed greater sense of dignity and worth.

Before Vatican II	After Vatican II
Local priest addressed only by surname; in some places his hand was kissed on meeting.	Priests addressed by first name; hand-kissing stopped.
Kneeling to the bishop and kissing his ring.	Obeisance to bishops stopped.

'**Holy death**' spirituality demanded that a priest should always be on call, to administer Last Rites.	Emphasis upon regular reception of Sacraments; and 'living' the Faith rather than dying in it.

The emphasis on the 'community' dimension of the liturgy, the dignity of the laity and parish pastoral life (the Church as the People of God) led to the development of parish pastoral councils, deanery councils and diocesan lay councils. On the parish level Catholics felt more involved with the introduction of parish newsletters and social clubs.

APPENDIX FIVE

RECUSANT TEACHING SONGS

The serious concern of the persecuted Catholic families of Elizabethan England and Wales, for the spiritual lives of their children, is well illustrated by the two following songs. The Recusant families were forbidden to teach their children the Catholic Faith; the penalty, if convicted of doing so, was life imprisonment (the Law was not repealed until 1791). Undeterred they found ways around the Penal laws, one of which was to compose teaching songs. These compositions, nowadays simply called 'traditional English songs' are still sung, but their history is not known to the general public.

The Twelve Days of Christmas	**Veiled meaning**
On the first day of Christmas, My true love sent to me A partridge in a pear tree.	'True love' refers to God.
On the second day of Christmas, My true love sent to me Two turtle doves, And a partridge in a pear tree.	Old and New Testaments.
On the third day of Christmas, My true love sent to me Three French hens… etc.	Theological virtues of Faith, Hope and Charity.
On the fourth day of Christmas, My true love sent to me Four calling birds … etc.	Four Gospels/Four Evangelists.

On the fifth day of Christmas,
My true love sent to me
Five golden rings ...
etc.

First Five Books of the Bible
The Pentateuch.

On the sixth day of Christmas
My true love sent to me
Six geese a-laying ...
etc.

The Six Days of Creation.

On the seventh day of Christmas
My true love sent to me
Seven swans a-swimming ...
etc.

The Seven Sacraments.

On the eight day of Christmas
My true love sent to me
Eight maids a-milking ...
etc.

The Eight Beatitudes.

On the ninth day of Christmas
My true love sent to me
Nine ladies dancing ...
etc.

Nine Fruits of Holy Spirit.

On the tenth day of Christmas
My true love sent to me
Ten lords a-leaping ...
etc.

The Ten Commandments.

On the eleventh day of Christmas
My true love sent to me
Eleven pipers piping ...
etc.

The Eleven faithful Apostles.

On the twelfth day of Christmas
My true love sent to me
Twelve drummers drumming ...
etc.

The twelve points of doctrine
in The Apostles' Creed.

While the song was used and passed on orally, it was first known to be published in 1780.

Green Grow the Rushes, O! | Veiled meaning

I'll sing you one, O
Green grow the rushes, O
What is your one, O?
One is one and all alone
And evermore shall be so.

    There is only One, everlasting and eternal God (rushes are evergreens).

I'll sing you two, O
Green grow the rushes, O
What are your two, O?
Two, two, the lily-white boys,
Clothed all in green, O
One is one and all alone
And evermore shall be so.

    Two Testaments in the Bible.

    Christ and John the Baptist baptising and baptised among the green rushes and lilies of the Jordan river.

I'll sing you three, O
Green grow the rushes, O
What are your three, O?
Three, three the rivals,
Two, two the lily-white boys,
Clothed all in green , O
One is one and all alone
And evermore shall be so.

    Persons of the Trinity.

    Obscure: could refer to three Synoptic Gospels.

I'll sing you four, O
Green grow the rushes, O
What are your four, O?
Four for the Gospel makers,
Three …
etc.

    The Four Gospels and evangelists.

I'll sing you five, O
Green grow the rushes, O
What are your five, O?
Five for the symbols at your door,
Four …
etc.

    A pentagram fixed to door – against evil spirits.

I'll sing you six, O …
Six for the six proud walkers,
Five …
etc.

    The original probably had 'waters' and referred to six water pots at wedding feast of Cana.

I'll sing you seven, O ...
Seven for seven stars in the sky,　　Seven gifts of the Holy Spirit that
Six ...　　　　　　　　　　　　　　overcome the seven deadly sins.
etc.

I'll sing you eight, O ...
Eight for eight bright shiners,　　　　　The eight Beatitudes.
Seven ...
etc.

I'll sing you nine, O ...
Nine for the nine bright rainers,　　(Different versions do not
Eight ...　　　　　　　　　　　　　　　　agree here).
etc.

Ten for the ten commandments ...　　The Ten Commandments

Eleven for the eleven who went　　　　The eleven Apostles
to heaven ...　　　　　　　　　　　　　without Judas.

Twelve for the twelve Apostles...　　The Twelve called by Jesus.

The Catholics of sixteenth and seventeenth-century England almost certainly adapted this song, for their teaching purposes, from a Jewish source, because the first recorded version of the song was in Hebrew. Readers may well know variants of the above song, because several versions are recorded and there is some lack of clarity in what has come down to us.

APPENDIX SIX

PATRON SAINTS

In a church building a statue or picture of a saint portrayed is not usually supplied with a name. We do not know what most of them looked like, so this presents a difficulty! However there is a long established practice or convention to assist recognition; symbols, or emblems, are used. For example, Mary, the Mother of God, is traditionally shown holding the Child Jesus. This ancient convention, established in the Eastern Church, has in modern times, been set aside by the representations, in the Western Church, of the Blessed Virgin arising from the apparitions at Lourdes. Fatima and La Salette etc (see Appendix Three).

Further examples: St Joseph is shown carrying carpenter's tools; St Christopher holds the Child Jesus on his left arm, while carrying a staff in his right hand; St Anthony of Padua is shown wearing a brown Franciscan habit and carrying the Child Jesus on his arm.

Not all saints have symbols; this is particularly true of modern saints, like St John Bosco, of whom we have photographs.

Occupation, etc	Patron Saint	Symbol
Accountants	Matthew	Winged man/purse
Actors	Genesius; Vitus	Sword
Advertising	Bernardine of Siena	Sun inscribed with iHs
Air travellers	Joseph of Cupertino	*none*
Altar servers	John Berchmans	Cross and rosary
Archers	Sebastian	Arrows
Architects	Thomas the Apostle	Set square and lance
Art	Catherine of Bologna	Artist's palette
Artists	Luke	Ox, book
Astronomers	Dominic	Rosary
Athletes	Sebastian	*above*

Authors	Francis de Sales	Open book
Bakers	Elizabeth of Hungary	Bread/flowers
Bankers	Matthew	*above*
Barbers	Cosmas and Damien	Box of ointment
Beggars	Alexius	Begging bowl
Blind, the	Raphael, the Archangel	Fish and staff
Blood banks	Januarius	*none*
Boatmen	Julian the Hospitaler	*none*
Bookbinders	Peter Celestine	*none*
Bookkeepers	Matthew	*above*
Booksellers	John of God	Crown of thorns
Boy Scouts	George	Dragon
Brewers	Augustine	Child/dove
Bricklayers	Stephen	Pile of rocks
Brides	Nicholas	Anchor/boat/three purses
Broadcasters	Gabriel, the Archangel	Angel with lily
Builders	Barbara	Cannon/chalice/tower
Butchers	Antony, hermit	Bell
Cab drivers	Fiacre	Carriage
Cancer patients	Peregrine Laziosi	Bandaged foot
Candlemakers	Bernard	Bees/pen
Canon lawyers	Raymond of Penafort	Scroll
Carpenters	Joseph	Carpenter's square
Catechists	Charles Borromeo	Host with ciborium
Catholic Press	Francis de Sales	*above*
Charitable groups	Vincent de Paul	Children
Child Birth	Gerald Majella	*none*
Children	Nicholas	*above*
Choirboys	Dominic Savio	Book and pen
Clergy	Gabriel, the Archangel	*above*
Cleaners, house	Martha	Dragon
Comedians	Vitus	Cockerel
Confessors	Alphonsus Liguouri	Book and pen
Cooks	Martha	*above*
Dancers	Vitus	*above*
Deaf, the	Francis de Sales	*above*
Dentists	Apollonia	*none*
Desperate situations	Jude	Club/Square rule
Dietitians	Martha	*above*
Dying, the	Joseph	*above*
Ecologists	Francis of Assisi	Birds/deer/stigmata

Editors	John Bosco	Photographs
Emigrants	Frances Xavier Cabrini	Photographs
Engineers	Ferdinand III	none
Entertainers	Cecilia	Organ
Epileptics	Dymphna	Sword & lamp
Europe	Benedict	Bell/crozier/raven
Expectant mothers	Gerald Majella	none
Eye sufferers	Lucy	Cord/eyes
Falsely accused	Raymond Nonnatus	none
Farmers	George	*above*
Fathers	Joseph	*above*
Firemen	Florian	none
Fire prevention	Barbara	*above*
First communicants	Tarsicius	Host with ciborium
Fishermen	Andrew	Transverse cross
Florists	Thérèse of Lisieux	Roses with a cross
Foresters	John Gualbert	none
Funeral directors	Joseph of Arimathea	Pot of oinment
Gardeners	Dorothy	Flowers
Girls	Agnes	Lamb
Glassworkers	Luke	*above*
Goldsmiths	Dunstan	Fire prongs
Greetings	Valentine	Heart
Grocers	Michael, the Archangel	Banner/dragon/scales
Hairdressers	Martin de Porres	Animals/sick person
Headaches	Teresa of Avila	Arrow/book
Heart patients	John of God	Crown of thorns
Hopeless causes	Jude	Boat/Axe
Hospital admin.	Basil the Great	Open book
Hospitals	Camillus de Lellis	none
Hoteliers	Amand	none
Housewives	Anne	Door
Immigrants	Frances Xavier Cabrini	*above*
Interracial justice	Martin de Porres	*above*
Jewellers	Dunstan	*above*
Journalists	Francis de Sales	*above*
Jurists	John Capistran	none
Labourers	Isidore	Bees/pen
Lawyers	Thomas More	Axe
Learning	Ambrose	Bees/dove
Librarians	Jerome	Lion

Locksmiths	Dunstan	*above*
Lost articles	Anthony of Padua	Christ child
Lovers	Valentine	Roses
Married women	Monica	*above*
Medical tech.	Albert the Great	Globe
Mentally ill	Dymphna	*none*
Merchants	Francis of Assisi	*above*
Messengers	Gabriel, the Archangel	*above*
Metalworkers	Eligius	Crozier
Midwives	Raymond Nonnatus	*none*
Missions	Francis Xavier	Bell/crucifix
Mothers	Monica	Girdle
Motorists	Christopher	Christ child
Mountaineers	Bernard of Menthon	*none*
Music/musicians	Cecilia	*above*
Nurses	Agatha	Bread
Nursing service	Elizabeth of Hungary	*above*
Orators	John Chrysostom	Bees/dove
Orphans	Jerome Emiliani	*none*
Painters	Luke	*above*
Paratroopers	Michael, the Archangel	*above*
Parish priests	John Vianney	Crucifix
Pediastry	Roche	Staff & dog
Pharmacists	Cosmas and Damien	*above*
Philosophers	Catherine of Alexandria	Wheel/lamb
Physicians	Luke	*above*
Pilgrims	James the Greater	Key/shell/staff
Pilots	Joseph of Cupertino	*none*
Plasterers	Bartholomew	Knife
Poets	Cecilia	*above*
Police	Michael, the Archangel	*above*
Poor, the	Anthony of Padua	*above*
Porters	Christopher	*above*
Postal workers	Gabriel, the Archangel	*above*
Preachers	Catherine of Alexandria	*above*
Pregnant women	Gerard Majella	*above*
Printers	Augustine	*above*
Prisoners	Barbara	above
Prisoners of war	Leonard	Chain
Public relations	Bernardine of Siena	*above*
Radiologists	Michael, the Archangel	*above*
Retreat preachers	Ignatius Loyola	Book/chasuble

Rheumatism sufferers	James the Greater	*above*
Road-crossing persons	Drogo	*none*
Sailors	Brendan	Leather boat
Scholars	Brigid	Candle/cross
Scientists	Albert the Great	*above*
Sculptors	Claude	*none*
Secretaries	Genesius	Sword
Seminarians	Charles Borromeo	*above*
Shepherds	Drogo	*none*
Shoemakers	Crispin	Boot/shoe
Sick, the	John of God	*above*
Singers	Cecilia	*above*
Skaters	Lidwina	*none*
Skiers	Bernard of Clairvaux	*above*
Skin diseases, sufferers from	Marculf	*none*
Social justice	Joseph	*none*
Social workers	Louise de Marillac	*none*
Soldiers	George	*above*
Speleonlogists	Benedict	*above*
Stonecutters	Clement	*none*
Stonemasons	Barbara	*above*
Students	Thomas Aquinas	Chalice/dove
Surgeons	Cosmas and Damien	*above*
Tax collectors	Matthew	*above*
Teachers	John Baptist de la Salle	*none*
Telecommunication workers	Gabriel, the Archangel	*above*
Theologians	Alphonsus Liguori	*above*
Throat infections	Blaise	Candle
Travelers	Christopher	*above*
Vocations	Alphonsus	*above*
Weavers	Anastasia	Cross/Jar
Widows	Paula	*none*
Winegrowers	Amand	*none*
Women in labour	Anne	*above*
Workers	Joseph	*above*
Writers	Francis de Sales	*above*
Yachtsmen	Adjutor	*none*
Youth	Aloysius Gonzaga	Crucifix & rosary

Personal Patron Saint: For hundreds of years Catholic parents named their child after one of the saints, so that the child had their own patron and heavenly intercessor, to whom they could turn for help. In fact in Catholic countries, like Poland, it was not the practice to keep birthdays (which were almost certainly not recorded anyway) but to annually keep the feast day of your patron saint. In recent times many Catholics have abandoned this ancient practice in favour of adopting the name of a current celebrity, or, in order to be different from others, a constructed name.

BIBLIOGRAPHY

Already Within. Daniel O'Leary, Columba Press, Blackrock, Dublin, 2000.
Catechism of the Catholic Church. Geoffrey Chapman, London, 1994.
Contemplation in a World of Action. Thomas Merton, Trustees of the Merton Legacy Trust, 1971.
Christian Spirituality. Alister E. McGrath, Blackwell, Oxford, 1999.
De tout Coeur. Papal address of Pope John Paul II, Paris, 1993.
Deus Caritas Est. Pope Benedict XVI, CTS, London, 2006.
Dictionary of Liturgy and Worship. ed. J.G. Davies, SCM Press, London, 1972x.
Discovering Saints in Britain. John Vince, Shire Publications, Aylesbury, 1969.
Documents of Vatican II. ed. Walter M. Abbott SJ, Geoffrey Chapman, London, 1966.
Edmund Campion. Evelyn Waugh, Image Books, New York, 1952.
From Age to Age. Edward Foley, Liturgy Training Publications, Chicago, 1991.
In God We Doubt. John Humphrys, Hodder & Stoughton, 2007.
Jesus of Nazareth. Pope Benedict XVI, Bloomsbury, London, 2007.
Let's Celebrate. Tony Castle, Hodder & Stoughton, London, 1984.
Letter and Spirit. Scott Hahn, Darton Longman and Todd, London, 2006.
Life of St Antony. St Athanasius, Select Works, vol. IV Nicene & Post-Nicene Fathers, Philip Schaff & Henry Wace, T.T. Clark, Edinburgh, 1987.

Living Faith. Creative Communications, Fenton, MO, USA.

Mary, Grace and Hope in Christ. ARCIC, Continuum, London, 2006.

Maze of Deception. Beverley Risdon, Journey into Wholeness, Colchester, 2007.

Megatrends 2000. J. Naisbitt, William Morrow & Co, New York, 1990.

Mystics of the Church. Evelyn Underhill, James Clarke, Cambridge, 1925.

Oxford Dictionary of the Christian Church. ed. Cross & Lawrence, Oxford, 3rd edition, 2005.

One Bread One Body. Catholic Bishops' Conference of England and Wales, CTS, London, 1998.

Prayer of the Heart. George Maloney SJ, Ave Maria Press, Indiana, USA, 1981.

Sacramentum Caritati. Pope Benedict XVI, CTS, London, 2007.

Spiritual Exercises of St Ignatius, trans and commentary. George Ganss SJ. Loyola Press, Chicago, 1992.

Story of A Soul, St Thérèse of Lisieux. ICS Publications, Washington, 1996.

Streams of Living Water. Richard Foster, Eagle, Trowbridge, 1999.

The Fire and the Cloud. Anthology: ed. David Fleming, Geoffrey Chapman, London, 1978.

The Gift of Scripture. Catholic Bishops' Conference of England and Wales, CTS, London, 2005.

The Image of Christ. Catalogue of Exhibition, 'Seeing Salvation' National Gallery, London, 2000.

The Life of Thomas More. Peter Ackroyd, Chatto & Windus, London, 1998.

The Perfection of Love. Anthology: ed. Tony Castle, Collins, London, 1986.

The Stripping of the Altars. Eamon Duffy, Yale University Press, London, 1992.

The Spiritual Life. A. Tanquerey, Desclee, Tournai, Belgium, 1930.
The Spiritual Life. Evelyn Underhill, Morehouse, Ontario, Canada, 1985.
The Interpretation of Scripture. Pontifical Biblical Commission, presented to Pope John Paul II, April 1993.
With the Word of God. Jude Groden RSM, Christopher O'Donnell, O.Carm., McCrimmons, Great Wakering, 2003.

INDEX

A
Adoration 85-88, 90, 93 131, 168, 176
Advent 140
Aid to the Church in Need 156
Alb 134, 165
Altar 21, 35-42, 85
Ambo 21, 44, 165
Angelus 104, 166
Antony, St 46
ARCIC 121, 166
Ash Wednesday 139, 166
Athanasius, St 46
Augustine of Canterbury, St 54
Augustine of Hippo, St 52
Augustianian Canons 134, 169

B
Baptism 30, 72-83, 138
Baptistery 72, 76, 167
Beatles, The 24
Benedict Labre, St 87
Benedict XVI, Pope 27, 56, 59, 74, 129, 143, 159
Benediction 85, 90, 131, 168
Benedictines 49, 167
Bernard of Clairvaux, St 95
Bernardette, St 112-13
Bible 29, 47-64, 168
Bonaventure, St 127

C
Cafod 156-7, 169
Canons 169
Canonisation 123
Caritas Network 158
Carthusians 128, 169
Catacombs 36-38, 118
Cathedra 65, 68 170
Catholic Socialism 163
Celebrant's chair 65
Celtic spirituality 78, 150
Charismatic Renewal Movement 149
Children of Mary 146-7
Christmas 134, 137
Church 15, 21, 28, 171
Communion of Saints 115
Confessional 78, 80, 171
Collins, Catherine 17, 163
Confraternity 129, 130, 172
Congregation 99, 172
Constantine, Emperor 37
Contemplation 50-51, 159-60

Corpus Christi 129, 173
Creation spirituality 150
Creed, Apostles' 117, 125
Cross 94-101, 115
Crucifix 94-101, 173

D
de Chardin, Teilhard 150, 199
de Foucauld, Charles 87
Desert Fathers 46, 49, 173
Devotia Moderna 50, 174
Discipleship 26-28
Divine Revelation 58
Divine Mercy 151-2
Doctor of the Church 174
Dominic Barberi, Bl 99
Duff, Frank 148, 199
Dura Europas 35

E
Easter 29, 136
   Candle (Paschal) 77, 138
   Triduum 139, 184
   Vigil 77, 138, 140
Edict of Milan 37
Edmund Campion, St 41
Eucharist 35-43
Epiphany 147
Eudists 132
Exercises, Spiritual
   see Spiritual Exercises
Exposition 89-91, 93, 168, 175

F
Fasting 139
Fatima 20, 222
Faustina, Maria St 151-53
First Friday 129, 131, 174
Five Wounds of Christ 96-7
Font 72, 174
Forty Hours 90, 92, 176
Forty Martyrs 42
Francis de Sales, St 71, 129, 132
Francis of Assisi, St 69, 96
Franciscan Order 127, 176
Frederick Ozanam, Bl 162-163

G
Good Friday 139, 176
Gospel 48
Gothic Revival 16
Green Scapular 149

Guard of Honour 130, 131
Guigo II 49

H
Hail Mary 108, 177
Happy Death 108
Harrington, Wilfrid 60
Hilton, Walter 174
Holy Death Spirituality 177
Holy Water 177
Holy Week 137, 139, 178
Homily 48
House Churches 35-6

I
Icons 108, 173, 178
Ignatius of Loyola, St 51, 179
Immaculate Medal 146-8
Incarnation 29, 136
Indulgences 178
Indwelling Christ 30
Inspiration of Scripture 57
Intercession to saints 116-21

J
Jerome, St 62-64
John Eudes, St 128, 132-133
John Paul II, Pope 31, 57, 122-4
John, the Evangelist 38, 62, 205, 210
John Vianney, St 81-5
Jesuits 51, 128, 179
Julian of Norwich 97, 174, 179
Justine Bisqueburu 149

L
Labore, St Catherine 147-8
Lady chapel 103, 104
Lamy, Madeleine 132
Lay Apostolate 148
Lectio Divina 49, 127
Lectern 21, 180
Lectionary 47
Legion of Mary 148
Lent 134, 138-9
Leo XIII, Pope 131
Little Way Association 157
Little Way of St Thérèse 32
Liturgical colours 134
Liturgical Year 134-8
Liturgy 141, 145, 146
Lourdes 20, 112-14, 222

M
Margaret Cavendish, Duchess 115
Margaret Clitherow, St 40-1
Margaret Mary, St 128-9, 133, 146
Martyrs, Early 36
Martyrs, English 40-2, 89

Mary, Blessed Virgin 103-14
Mass 17, 21, 35, 180
Maundy Thursday 69, 139, 180
McDonagh, Sean 151
Meditation 49-51
Merton, Thomas 160
Minister 69
Miraculous Medal 147-8
Monastery 180
Monstrance 168, 181
Moore, John 18
Mystics
    medieval 96, 127, 128, 133
    English 96, 127, 128, 174

N
Newman, John Henry, Cardinal 20, 163
Nicholas, St
    see Santa Claus
Novena 181

O
O'Donohue, John 150
Oratorians 131
Our Lady
    see Mary, Blessed Virgin

P
Palm Sunday 139
Paschal candle
    see Easter candle
Passionists 98
Patron saints 119
Paul Danei 97
Paul, St 36, 38, 59, 61, 116, 127
Paul VI, Pope 179
Penance *see* Reconciliation
Pius V, Pope 135, 177
Pius IX, Pope 149
Pius X, Pope 79, 177
Pius XII, Pope 129, 148
Presider's chair
    see Celebrant's chair
Presbytery 181
Priory 181
Pugin, Augustus 15, 16
Pulpits 44
Pursuivants 42

Q
Quant'Ore
    see Forty Hours

R
Real Presence 38-40
Reconciliation 76-83, 171
Reconciliation room 80, 171
Recusant 41, 182

Relics 37, 182
Rerodos 65, 85, 182
Reservation 88
Resurrection 29
Retreats 183
Rolle, Richard 175
Roman Missal 135
Roman Persecution 36
Rosary 104, 109, 183

S
Sacraments 29, 184
Sacra Triduum
  see Easter Triduum
Sacred Heart of Jesus 126-34, 146
Sacring, the 85
Saint 115-18
Sanctuary 134, 185
Santa Claus 142-4
Scapular 185
Scripture, Holy 44-58, 173
Second Vatican Council 11, 19, 47-48, 54, 58, 67, 79, 87, 91, 98, 116, 120, 131, 135, 146, 148, 157, 179
Sedilia 21, 185
Seminary 132-3, 185
Shema 58
Sign of the Cross 80, 98, 185
Sisters of the Refuge 133
Society of Jesus
  see Jesuits
Spiritual Director 186
Spiritual Exercises 52
Spirituality 9, 12, 22, 24, 145, 179

Stations of the Cross 139, 176, 186
Stigmata 96-7, 187
Stoup, water 80, 187
Suenans, Card. Leo 150
Sunday 135, 137
SVP 156-57, 188
Synoptic Gospels 62, 188

T
Tabernacle 85, 88, 89, 93, 188
Theotokos 107, 111, 113
Thérèse of Lisieux, St 31-2, 174, 199
Transubstantiation 39, 86, 189

U
Underhill, Evelyn 26, 161

V
Valentine, St 126
Villa Anaplaga 35
Vilnuis image 145
Vincent de Paul, St 162
Visitation Order 129, 132
Vulgate 64

W
Walsingham 103-4, 109, 189
Waugh, Evelyn 41
Way of the Cross
  see Stations of the Cross
Welborn, Amy 27
Wojtyla, Karol
  see John Paul II, Pope

ACKNOWLEDGEMENTS

1. *Streams of Living Water*, Richard Foster, Eagle, Trowbridge, 1999.
2. *Christian Spirituality*, Alister E. McGrath, Blackwell, Oxford, 1999.
3. *Deus Caritas Est*, Pope Benedict XVI, CTS, London, 2006.
4. *Story of Soul*, autobiography of St Thérèse of Lisieux; ICS Publications, Washington, 1996.
5. *Sacramentum Caritati*, Pope Benedict XVI, CTS, London, 2007.
6. *Mystics of the Church*, Evelyn Underhill, James Clarke, Cambridge, 1925.
7. *The Oxford Dictionary of the Christian Church*, Ed. Cross and Livingstone, 3rd edition 2005, Oxford.
8. *The Spiritual Life*, A. Tanquerey, Desclee Tournai, Belgium, 1930.
9. *The Spiritual Life*, Evelyn Underhill, Morehouse Ontario, Canada, 1985.
10. *Jesus of Nazareth*, Pope Benedict XVI, Bloomsbury, London, 2007.
11. *The Perfection of Love*, Anthology, Ed. Tony Castle, Collins, London, 1986.
12. *The Fire and the Cloud*, Anthology, Ed. David Fleming, Geoffrey Chapman, London, 1978.
13. *The Gift of Scripture*, Catholic Bishops' Conference of England and Wales, CTS, London, 2005.
14. *De tout Coeur*, Address of Pope John Paul II, 1993.
15. *From Age to Age*, Edward Foley, Liturgy Training Publications, Chicago, 1991.
16. *One Bread, One Body*, Catholic Bishops' Conference of England and Wales, CTS, London, 1998.
17. The Documents of Vatican II, Ed. Walter M. Abbott SJ., Geoffrey Chapman, London, 1966.

18. *With the Word of God: Lectio Divina*, Jude Groden RSM and Christopher O'Donnell O.Carm., McCrimmons, 2003.
19. *The Stripping of the Altars*, Eamon Duffy, Yale University Press, London, 1992.
20. *The Image of Christ*, Catalogue of the exhibition 'Seeing Salvation' at National Gallery, London, 2000.
21. *Catechism of the Catholic Church*, Geoffrey Chapman, London, 1994.
22. *The Tablet* article 'Made in the Marian Way', 16 June 2007 by Dr Eamon Duffy.
23. *Mary, Grace and Hope in Christ* (The Seattle Statement) ARCIC, Continuum, London, 2006.
24. *Discovering Saints in Britain*, John Vince, Shire Publications Ltd, Aylesbury, 1969.
25. *Prayer of the Heart*, George Maloney, Ave Maria Press, Indiana, 1981.
26. *A Dictionary of Liturgy and Worship*, Ed. J.G. Davies, SCM Press Ltd, London, 1972.
27. *In God We Doubt*, John Humphrys, Hodder and Stoughton, 2007.
28. *The Interpretation of the Bible in the Church*, Pontifical Biblical Commission.
29. *Letter and Spirit*, Scott Hahn, Darton Longman and Todd, London, 2006.
30. *Let's Celebrate*, Tony Castle, Hodder and Stoughton, London, 1984.
31. *Megatrends 2000*, J Naisbitt & P. Aburdene, William Morrow & Co., New York, 1990.
32. *Maze of Deception*, Beverley Risdon, Journey into Wholeness, Colchester, 2007.
33. *Contemplation in a World of Action*, Thomas Merton, Trustees of the Merton Legacy Trust, 1971.
34. *The Life of Thomas More*, Peter Ackroyd, Chatto & Windus, London, 1998.